THE ART OF REST

HOW SHABBAT CAN CHANGE YOUR LIFE

Rabbi Jeff Friedlander

Ivory Rook Publishing
Birmingham, AL

Copyright

The Art of Rest: How Shabbat Can Change Your Life by Rabbi Jeff Friedlander

Copyright ©2022 all rights reserved. No part of this book may be used or reproduced by any means, graphic, electronic, or mechanical, including photocopying, recording, taping or by any information storage retrieval system without the written permission of Ivory Rook Publishing™ and Jeff Friedlander, except in the case of brief quotations embodied in critical articles and reviews.
This book is a work of non-fiction. Registered trademarks and service marks are the property of their respective owners.

Cover Photograph: kwasny222 Image ID: 406366416
Edited by: Sherri Friedlander and Sally Herring
Library Cataloging Data
Names: Friedlander, Jeff (Jeff Friedlander) 1967 -
Title: *The Art of Rest: How Shabbat Can Change Your Life* / Rabbi Jeff Friedlander
5.5 in. × 8.5 in. (13.97 cm × 21.59 cm)
Description: Ivory Rook Publishing digital eBook edition | Ivory Rook Publishing print edition | Alabama: Ivory Rook Publishing, 2020-2022. P.O Box 1774 Alabaster, AL 35007

Summary: What is greater than sleep? Rest. In the busyness of the modern world true rest is rarely found. Good news! There is a way to have restorative, refreshing rest. In this book you will learn how G-d designed a weekly, monthly, and annual calendar so we can be full of energy and passion as we work and live.
Following the pattern of our designer, this book will give you the Biblical plan, historical realities, and modern path to real, genuine, G-d ordained REST. Take your life back as you discover The Art of Rest that lies in Shabbat!

ISBN-13: 978-1-949184-83-9 (eBook) | 978-1-949184-78-5 (print) |

1. Sabbath 2. Rest 3. Motivational 4. Jewish 5. Christian 6. Leadership 7. History

Printed in the United States of America

THE ART OF REST

Rabbi Jeff Friedlander

Acknowledgements

I wrote a book. Not an original by any means for under heaven there is nothing original. I must acknowledge that the words in this book are the culmination of thousands of years of other people's work, training, writing, teaching, and giving. I have learned from so many great minds and passionate lovers of Messiah that to try and name them would leave some out and others insulted. I therefore simply say to all who have contributed to my growth as a man and minister, thank you!

Specifically, I can't say thank you enough to Sherri Friedlander and Sally Herring for their countless hours of reading, editing, challenging, correcting, and encouraging of me and the text. They have gone beyond the call of duty and without them this book would not have been written.

I also want to thank Gene Rowley. You are not only a great friend, or dare I say family brother, but your passion for writing and publishing made me want to finish this book. Thank you for the gift.

I could list so many people who have helped me in this process of being a writer and finishing this work but I am afraid I would leave someone out. I simply say thank you.

Most importantly, I thank G-d Almighty for His gracious love and patience with me. He has guided, chided, and discipled me with love. This love has now become my heart. Should you read anything true and good in the book it most certainly comes from Him. The other stuff comes from me. He is the author and finisher of our faith and in that way, He is the author of the good parts of this work.

Dedication

I dedicate this work to G-d, my wife, Sherri, and my family. I have been blessed to have a faithful watcher in my life. My wife has been dedicated and loyal when many would have headed for the hills. She has remained constant in her covenant, her love, and her devotion. She has challenged me, encouraged me, pushed me, and reminded me of the calling that G-d has put on my life. I am forever grateful for her in more ways than my words can express. This book would never have happened had it not been for her. We have built a life together and this journey into Shabbat is one of the great joys we have experienced. Thank you, my love! We got history!

To my children and their families, I pray that this book will be a legacy of truth that you use to help build your own Biblical customs. May you always remember that I love each of you with my whole heart and desire nothing but G-d's best for you. May His Shabbat rest be your reality!

PREFACE

I was born a Jew. I accepted Yeshua (Jesus) as Messiah when I was in college. I went to church on Sunday. I read the Old and New Testament. I went to ministry school and became an ordained pastor in a Christian church. I went to Messianic Yeshiva and became an ordained Rabbi in a Messianic Jewish congregation. I was an owner in a couple of businesses and an employee for a moderate size corporation. Each of these experiences and studies has been used by G-d to shape my worldview and the way I read THE BOOK. I am passionate about many things and one of them is Shabbat. Yet, for so many years, I did not see the power of this great truth of the Bible.

This book is my attempt to share my journey and that of many others who have discovered the power of Shabbat. In this book you will read the Biblical theology of Shabbat and may be surprised at what is written. We will look at the history of Shabbat throughout the times of the Hebrew scriptures (Old Testament), the New Testament, and the post New Testament period. We will see how traditions changed and which traditions are based on the scriptures. Most importantly, this book is written as a call to a generation divided but longing for unity.

My heart and passion are for the body of Messiah—Jew and Gentile--to be one as Yeshua (Jesus) prayed in **John 17:20-21**:

I pray not on behalf of these only, but also for those who believe in Me through their message, that they all may be one. Just as You, Father, are in Me and I am in You, so also may they be one in Us, so the world may believe that You sent Me.

Unity among Jews and non-Jews who are followers of Messiah Yeshua is what will bring credibility to the gospel itself.

Paul, the apostle, writes that Jews and Gentiles are both to be grafted into the "olive tree." This tree represents the proverbial "tree of life" and the unity that comes from knowing the Messiah and having one's sins atoned for. The olive tree is nourished by the Jewish root. This Jewish root has many modern and ancient traditions attached to it. However, there is a much greater command that is not just Jewish. In fact, it is Biblical and Hebraic. That command is the guarding and keeping of Shabbat.

As you read this book may it be a light to your path and inspire you to the Rest that G-d has for you. May this be the beginning of your great life-long practice of Shabbat.

I want to define some terms that are used in this book. We use the Hebrew name for Jesus, which is Yeshua, throughout most of the book. We use several names for G-d, including Yehovah, Yahweh, Adonai, G-d, Elohim, and L-rd. The true name of G-d, the one He called himself in the Bible, is spelled with four Hebrew letters: יְהוָה Depending on which vowels are inputted, the pronunciation changes. Since this book is not about how to pronounce the name of G-d, we will use several names. But know this: Those four letters are the NAME of G-d and He has it in His Bible over 6800 times. That name is THE NAME!

I hyphenate the name G-d and L-rd throughout the book. See Appendix C for the explanation.

I use interchangeably the word Shabbat (Hebrew) and Sabbath (English).

I sometimes refer to Jewish people, including myself as the Jews, or a Jew. This is in no way meant as derogatory and should be taken in the spirit in which it is written and that is a shortened version of Jewish.

The word "church" does not appear in the Bible manuscripts. The original Greek word was Ekklesia and means "called out ones, called out to rule."

See Appendix C for a larger list of Hebrew words and definitions.

We use the Tree of Life version for scriptures unless otherwise noted.

Rabbi Jeff Friedlander

INTRODUCTION

He wakes at 6:00 A.M. and already feels behind. He knows the roads are jammed with traffic and his responsibilities at the office start the minute he crawls out of bed. Actually, they had never stopped. In fact, often this thought makes him want to remain in bed. He comforts himself with an idea: "Maybe if I don't get up, I will not have to face the day or myself. Maybe I can lay here and hide from the world and the family and run from the work that has become my life. Maybe…," and then the snooze button releases and the alarm sounds for the third time and the dream ends.

As he splashes water on his face and begins to shave, he looks in the mirror at the shell of man he has become. He sees a face worn with the aging that comes with stress and deadlines. The once young and hopeful skin has become tainted and discolored. The eyes that once burned with fire are now barely open. Although in years he is still counted as young, not even middle aged, he feels as though his life is slipping away. But enough of that. "I must hurry," he tells himself. "Work cannot wait and with all the bills to pay and the goals to accomplish I have no time to reflect and relax." So, he shaves, showers, and runs into high gear to get the job done until the end of the day.

Maybe this is how you have felt? Maybe your circumstances are different, but the emotion is the same? The cares of this world seem to be overwhelming an entire society these days. However, that is not the intent G-d has for His people.

There is a rest that is better than you can imagine. G-d created a way for each person to have a weekly recharge as he renews his commitment and covenant.

The idea and implementation of resting on the seventh day of the week began in the heart and actions of G-d Himself. He created the universe and all that we have and are. He created a pattern for us to follow for our benefit. Over the millennia many things have changed as mankind took matters into their own hand. But what would it be like if we all decided to follow the ancient path, to walk in the pattern of our creator?

This book is about discovering the Biblical solution to the busyness and chaos that life seems to be producing. Shabbat is a great gift to mankind.

Shabbat was given to mankind as a gift and a requirement. G-d knows how we are made, physically, emotionally, and spiritually. When acting within His design we thrive.

In the first part of this book, I present the Biblical case for a seventh day Shabbat. I take you through the many passages and examples given in the Bible of defining and obeying the fourth commandment. I then show how mankind took G-d's simple command and changed it to fit a different way of life. The second part of the book will guide you into true rest. You will discover that G-d's gift is not bondage to a rule of suffering but rather freedom and rejuvenation. In this part of the book, you will find the way back to His ancient path.

This book is a book of passion and timeliness. Some of the questions I began to ask G-d formed the basis of this book. Does it matter what day I rest as long as I rest at least one day? Does it matter if I call my day of rest Shabbat or not? Is it wrong to take Saturday as a day of rest rather than Sunday? Is this a Jewish idea anyway and therefore does not affect the Gentile church goer? What is rest? What is work?

Some other related questions I tackle in this book: What is Shabbat? Is Shabbat for today? How did Yeshua and the disciples practice Shabbat? Are Gentiles supposed to keep Shabbat? Isn't Shabbat part of the law of Moses and are New Testament believers free from that law? What was the culture, tradition, and structure of the first century community of faith? Could Shabbat really be lifechanging? Is it possible that simply rearranging our schedule to uphold a true Shabbat could make a difference? In fact, does G-d even care?

What you are reading is a guidebook to the greatest secret that most followers of Yeshua have not yet fully seen. This book unlocks the door and removes the barrier to the blessing that awaits on the other side of Shabbat. If you dare to read it be forewarned that G-d will give you access and then hold you accountable for what He has entrusted to you. Read on and capture the command to guard and keep rest. Your life will never be the same.

Contents

Part I: A Biblical Foundation

Part II: Restoring Rest

SHABBAT CHANGED MY WORLD

I am Jewish. For most, that would make it easy to understand why I would write a book on the Shabbat. Most believe Shabbat is a Jewish tradition and since I am Jewish it makes sense for me to practice my faith this way. However, neither of those last two statements is true. Later in this book, I will expand the Shabbat being a biblical holiday rather than a Jewish holiday. For now, I want to set the record straight on Jewish identity.

I did not have to do anything to be Jewish. I was born a Jew. I did not earn it nor convert to become a Jew. I just simply am. Being Jewish does not mean that I practice Judaism. Judaism is a faith; Jewish is an ethnicity. My dad is Jewish, (my mother is not and there are some sects of Judaism which define your ethnicity by your mother only) as were both of his parents and all his grandparents, however they stopped attending weekly Shabbats before he was a teenager. When my dad was 21 years old, he became friends with a protestant Christian who took my dad to church. My dad decided that he wanted to be a follower of Yeshua (Jesus). When he became a Christian in the 1950's there were no messianic synagogues to attend. There were no places to keep Jewish traditions and believe that Yeshua was the Messiah. He went to the church world leaving many of his Jewish customs behind, including the practice of attending services on Saturday rather than Sunday.

When I was born, my family was fully engaged in the church world. I am Jewish by blood. However, my only connection to my Jewish roots culturally was the occasional visit with my Jewish grandparents who gave me the traditional Hanukkah gelt (gold covered chocolate coins). Our regular faith life was the protestant church world.

We stopped attending regular services when I was in the ninth grade. It wasn't until my junior year in college that I had an encounter with Yeshua and became a born-again believer in the promised Jewish Messiah. My hunger for the word of G-d in the Bible was awakened and I studied for hours absorbing the truth I found there. I grew in my faith alongside my future bride.

We served in the local *Ekklesia* (called out ones commonly called church) in many capacities, raised four children in the Christian faith and it seemed as if everything in our faith world was on point.

I began to have an unsettled feeling about our time at the large church where we served. We, my wife, and I, always had been drawn in our hearts and souls to the Hebrew scriptures (Old Testament). We loved to study and read all the wonderful psalms and history. The prophets raised so many questions and Genesis was my favorite book. We had been serving in a wonderful church that was big and doing amazing work, but we had an increasing feeling that our time there was up. We were becoming more dissatisfied each year. This was no fault of the church but rather what G-d was doing to prepare us for what was to come.

After being married just shy of 20 years, G-d began to move in His mysterious ways. In mid-summer of 2010, three people in different areas of our life randomly asked me if I was Jewish. My confirming answer elicited an invitation to a Messianic Jewish Synagogue in my town. I was unfamiliar with this form of Judaism, but something in my spirit was sparked. As I investigated it, I discovered that the Messianic Jewish movement had been growing around the world for over 100 years.[1] As a Jewish man, living my faith walk in the church, I was unaware this movement existed. Since then, I have learned I was not alone in my ignorance. Few people in the modern church world are aware of Messianic Judaism.

Well, when three different people come to you in one week with the same question you must take notice that G-d may be trying to get your attention. I followed the spiritual nudge and attended the synagogue for the first time in my life.

I knew that something there was speaking to me. I went back another time or two and attended a Bible study. I then went to a Friday night Shabbat service. Here, finally, was the breath of air my lungs had been craving for years. Here I heard the ancient sounds of the shofar and the chants of my Jewish people. These chants were ones that Yeshua himself may have said when He was in the temple or the synagogue. Some of these sounds went back to Ezra and Nehemiah's day. We were truly on ancient paths, and I was awed. I felt like I was home. From my childhood up until this moment I had been taught, trained, and heard the gospel and the teaching of the Bible only through protestant, western American eyes. For the first time, I was looking at the Bible through the eyes of those G-d chose to write it, the Jewish people. I was connecting to my heritage, and it was refreshing.

I wanted my family to come with me, however I had a hurdle to overcome. We had a tradition in our home that Friday night was our family night. Ironically, this proved to be our unintentional Shabbat, celebrated with pizza, movies, and root beer floats. I convinced them to give up just this one Friday night to attend the Friday night Shabbat service at the synagogue. Out of love and respect for me, they reluctantly attended and kept their lack of enthusiasm well concealed. As we encountered G-d and connected to our Jewish roots, this "one time" turned into our new family faith practice. We all began to serve and work in a messianic Jewish ministry as a family. In time, I became an ordained Rabbi. The joke in our home became, "We were just going to go one Friday...Now dad's a Rabbi."

My lack of interaction with Biblical Shabbat is not unique to many of you who read this book.

Shabbat in the Biblical worldview was not part of your training. In fact, most people, when they read the word "sabbath" in the Bible, immediately equate the word to "Sunday." During the last 2000 years, the Christian church has become so far removed from the idea of Sabbath that the word itself merely serves as a place marker for the day to attend church. This was my experience as well.

However, I have been transformed by experiencing the Biblical Shabbat. The Shabbat has become the central point of my practice of faith; a day of the week can seem so insignificant and yet it is so profound.

I am writing this book to two groups of people. The first group is the Jewish people. To all my Jewish *mishpocha* (family), I say thank you. The Jewish people have preserved the practice of Shabbat for thousands of years and passed that on to each generation. This is truly a gift from the Jews. I have a profound respect for the Jewish people as they have endured more than any culture in history. For the Jewish people to still be "a people" is a testimony to the covenant keeping power of our G-d.

However, in many ways my Jewish family has added many "fences" to the practice of Shabbat and from my perspective, confused the true power it holds. In this book, I hope my Jewish friends will find a refreshing breath of freedom from G-d in the keeping of Shabbat. Shabbat is so much more than rules created over the centuries. May you find joy unspeakable–and Biblical– as you discover the scriptural truth about Shabbat.

The practice of Shabbat is the gift of G-d to every person. The Jews were charged with sharing the gift. The Gentile world needed this command and traditional Jewish practices held it back from them. I write this book to you, my Jewish brothers, and sisters, so that you may remember the prophet Isaiah's words:

Isaiah 42:6

"I, Adonai, called You in righteousness, I will take hold of Your hand, I will keep You and give You as a covenant to the people, as a light to the nations...."

How can you be a light if you don't share Shabbat with the world? I am writing in hope that you will read and be inspired to share the gift of Shabbat with your Gentile friends that they may be nourished.

Second, I am writing to Gentile believers. Due to the church fathers divorce of Jewish practices, you have been denied a great gift. The Shabbat was given for all believers who follow the G-d of Abraham, Isaac, and Jacob, both Jew and Gentile. For nearly 2000 years, you have not had the privilege of really understanding or practicing the Biblical Shabbat. I hope the rest of this book will bring a great blessing to you as G-d reveals His commandment of keeping the Shabbat.

We are going look at the Biblical, historical, cultural, and traditional aspects of Shabbat. Join me as we discover the gift of G-d that is Shabbat.

Jeff Friedlander

THE SHABBAT PROMISE

Did you ever play the game hide and go seek as a child? What is so fascinating about *that* game? The one who is "it" is searching for the hidden players. G-d must be "it" because He is continually looking for us. He seeks us out to give to us His purpose and love. Many times, He is just waiting on us to seek Him as well.

Proverbs 23:23 we read:

It is to the glory of G-d to conceal a matter and to the glory of kings to search it out.

In order to restore the beauty of something lost we must seek out the matter as G-d gives it. Shabbat is a treasure that G-d possesses and wants us to seek and possess.

Great blessings dwell in the depths of His Words.

Psalm 91:1

He who dwells in the shelter of Elyon, will abide in the shadow of Shaddai.

When our search uncovers a hidden place, and we meet the L-rd there; we find great rest. Shabbat is a secret place, but it is so much more.

My friend Melvin discovered Shabbat and was kind enough to write his thoughts down for us:

As a Gentile follower of Yeshua, I have discovered the universal benefit of observing Sabbath."

The first Sabbath mentioned in scripture was the day following the creation of man. G-d did all the "work" and Adam had done nothing. By exploring some implications, we can begin to glean the meaning of true rest.

Many consider rest's purpose as recuperation from work. We see from this first day of rest in creation-- Adam had nothing from which to recover, but G-d provided for his rest.

SABBATH REST IS PROACTIVE, NOT REACTIVE.

If life was a symphony, Sabbath would be the rhythm section. Sabbath was G-d's gift to Adam and designed to be part of the productive cycle of life. As with any gift, a great way to express gratitude is to make use of gifts received.

SABBATH REST IS A REPEATED EXPRESSION OF GRATITUDE TO OUR CREATOR.

The gifts of life, work, and rest were given to Adam as a representative of all humanity. Sabbath is not a Jewish religious practice. It is a universal principle readily available to all to be equally received and practiced. Many cultures teach the importance of work, but neglect to model the vitality of rest.

SABBATH REST IS MY CONTRIBUTION TO THE BETTERMENT OF ALL MANKIND.

Melvin discovered the practice of Shabbat is not about observing a strict law of do's and don'ts, but rather a spirit of rest and holiness. This *moed* (appointed time) brings with it a special reward that cannot be planned or earned. Shabbat provides an intangible, non-quantifiable blessing. Our culture demands activity and constant attention to the work to be done seven days a week. Shabbat rest is an act of faith: We trust the pattern of G-d which allows for time to complete our workload in six days.

As I encounter believers who begin to view the scriptures with a more Hebraic understanding, one of the biggest questions I am asked about is Shabbat. It is understandable that Shabbat is surrounded by mystery because it has been buried under historical and religious rules and regulations, some purposefully designed to obscure the day, others effectively negating the joy of Shabbat.

Let's begin seeking then by looking at the past. Over the last 1800 years the Christian church has defined the day, the time, and the way in which worship is conducted. Shabbat on the other hand, had been observed by the Jewish community, and the Gentiles amongst us, for thousands of years when *Yeshua* came to earth. They followed the instructions from Genesis before there was a distinction of Jew and Gentile.

However, over the years the Jewish leaders had added rules and regulations to the practice of Shabbat. Yeshua confronted the Pharisees many times about their man-made rules and the burden it put on the people, but He did not speak against Shabbat itself, in its intended and pure form. As Gentile believers were coming into the faith of the promised Jewish Messiah, many conflicts arose among the Jewish believers in Messiah about how the Gentiles should practice faith in the Jewish Messiah. These tensions grew and practices of faith began to move further and further away from the Jewish expression and become a more Gentile style expression. In 325 C.E., The emperor of Rome, Constantine, intentionally and forcefully divorced the church from anything that resembled a Jewish practice. Shabbat was a casualty. It was legally mandated that observance would take place on Sunday, instead of the Biblical seventh day. The practice of Sabbath on Sunday was justified by a distortion and misapplication of Yeshua's words:

Mark 2:27

And he said to them, "The Sabbath was made for man, not man for the Sabbath.

The rest, as they say is history. Later in this book we will go into detail about the changes that took place and the results of those changes. Today, although each branch of Christianity may differ in the practice of Shabbat, one consistency is that Shabbat is Sunday. The Sunday Sabbath culture teaches that, "Shabbat was made for man," and therefore concludes that man can define Shabbat. As we examine Biblical teachings on Shabbat, we will discover that man is not given the right or authority to change the expressed written will and plan of G-d. There are many things that G-d gives man the freedom to express uniquely, for example, love, worship, and faith itself. However, when a plain command is given, we must resist the desire to change it for our own reasons or convenience.

Shabbat is a promise that when fulfilled unlocks hidden wonders. Through Shabbat we understand how G-d organizes the universe, the earth, the spiritual world, and our very bodies. We were created in His image and that has been marred and lost in many ways. We must understand how G-d operates to recapture the image in which He created us.

Yeshua confirms that there are hidden secrets and mysteries awaiting our discovery.

Matthew 7:7-8

Ask, and it will be given to you; seek, and you will find; knock, and it will be opened to you. For everyone who asks receives, and the one who seeks finds, and to the one who knocks it will be opened.

Our creator has a sense of mystery about Him. He seems to enjoy hiding aspects of Himself and invites us to search for Him.

Diamonds are rare and difficult to find. They take ages of immense pressure to create and years of searching to be mined. These precious stones provide beauty and enjoyment to the possessor. G-d wants us to find the diamonds of His ways and His word.

I have come to understand over the three plus decades of walking with Him that He is not hiding things from us for the sake of cruelty, nor is He playing a game. He is hiding them because the process of discovery is one of the ways we grow in the journey and get to know G-d. What a blessing!

However, to discover the "diamonds" we must uncover some secrets and remove some barriers or blocks that are in the way. There are patterns in the Bible that reveal the way in which we should "walk" out our faith. These patterns are discovered as we dig deeper for the gems. One of the most magnificent gems has been covered entirely for almost 2000 years. It is Shabbat. This gem reveals fresh understandings and blessings to those who follow where it leads.

Please do not misunderstand me. This is not some magic button you push, and suddenly G-d becomes your bell hop to give to you all you wish. G-d is not to be mocked for He is our creator and our G-d. However, this priceless jewel of Shabbat unlocks an understanding into G-d and His ways. When we follow His ways, we can then expect good things to happen and have peace to manage the bad things that happen.

Look at this passage from the Hebrew prophet Isaiah and be in awe at the power of the revelation of Shabbat.

Isaiah 56:1-2

*Here is what Adonai says: "Observe justice, do what is right, for my salvation is close to coming, my righteousness to being revealed." Happy is the person who does this, anyone who grasps it firmly, **who keeps Shabbat and does not profane it, and keeps himself from doing any evil.*** (emphasis mine)

People have searched for happiness in many ways over the span of history. They have searched for joy in careers, religious services, family. Books have been written, conferences attended and lots of money spent to find happiness. What if happiness was linked to something as simple as Shabbat? I know that you may be thinking, "this is not possible." But why not? The prophet Isaiah, whom G-d used to pen His word makes this link.

In the middle of the verse, he also lets us know that salvation is soon to come. Isaiah gives us a prophetic picture of the coming of Yeshua, the Hebrew word for salvation is יְשׁוּעָה Yeshua. This word is used all throughout the Hebrew scriptures, Tanakh. (See Appendix C for meaning of Tanakh)

He shows us a part of the hidden mystery: Messiah and Shabbat are connected in the treasure of happiness. In other words, Shabbat matters.

A little further, in **Isaiah Chapter 56 verses 6-8**, we see another treasure:

*And the foreigners who join themselves to Adonai to serve him, to love the name of Adonai, and to be his workers, **all who keep Shabbat and do not profane it, and hold fast to my covenant**, I will bring them to my holy mountain and make them joyful in my house of prayer; their burnt offerings and sacrifices will be accepted on my altar; for my house will be called a house of prayer for all peoples." Adonai Elohim says, he who gathers Isra'el's exiles: "There are yet others I will gather, besides those gathered already.*(emphasis mine)

Here Isaiah makes the bold statement that Shabbat is for more than just the Jews. Shabbat is an invitation to the nations. The promise extends to all people of all nations. Ascend the Holy Mountain of Adonai to become joyful in the house of prayer. There, sacrifices will be accepted in a house for all peoples.

Notice also, that Isaiah used the fourth commandment in this powerful announcement. He chose the fourth commandment as a link to the future. Do not miss that point. We must see the power here. The L-rd, through the prophet, is telling us that we must never exclude the nations from the gift of Shabbat. Salvation, Jews and Gentiles as one, and Shabbat are all connected.

Gentiles must never say they are not part of the kingdom of G-d or connected to the Jewish people. In fact, Paul speaks of this in the New Testament when he refers to Gentile and Jewish unity in Messiah as "one new man." [1]

Imagine for a moment how unity among those of the faith could begin on a day instituted in the creation account of the book of Genesis. As you read through this book you will see the pieces of this puzzle come together.

Isaiah is the very passage that Yeshua (Jesus) quotes from when he turns over the tables at the Temple:

Matthew 21:12-13

Yeshua entered the Temple grounds and drove out those who were doing business there, both the merchants and their customers. He upset the desks of the moneychangers and knocked over the benches of those who were selling pigeons. He said to them, "It has been written, 'My house will be called a house of prayer.' But you are turning it into a den of robbers!" (emphasis mine)

The context of his statement is that the foreigner could keep the Sabbath and not profane it. The house of prayer Yeshua refers to is the place where Jews and Gentiles both sacrifice, seek and worship G-d.

Finally, we see that by keeping the Shabbat, the foreigner can bring his sacrifices to Adonai and they will be accepted. This is good news for both Jews and Gentiles. Hear the good news from the prophet Isaiah, all people will be invited to come to the Holy Mountain of G-d and their sacrifices will be accepted and their prayers will be heard. We can understand this as a literal picture at the end of days when Messiah returns and there is a new heaven and a new earth and a new Jerusalem which He rules in. But we can also understand that the words of Isaiah are meant for us to realize that Shabbat is not to be put on the sideline in the practice of our faith. It is front and center. Shabbat is not just suggested nor removed from G-d's ways but rather is commanded to be applied to our lives.

This prophetic chapter of Isaiah--speaking to the future reign of the Messiah and the nations with him--is marked distinctly by the practice of Shabbat. Just in these verses we see three diamonds that come from delving deeply into the meaning of Shabbat. We become happy, foreigners are part of the house of prayer and our sacrifices are acceptable to G-d.

What does G-d treasure?

In Matthew chapter 6, Yeshua gives what is known as the Sermon on the Mount. This sermon is one of the seminal moments in his ministry. This teaching is a *midrash* (short teaching / explanation) in which He is sums up and clarifies parts of the Torah. During the teaching he makes some statements about money.

Matthew 6:24

You cannot serve G-d and mammon.

Yeshua carefully chose an important word in his sermon. Rather than saying 'money' He chose the word 'mammon.' Mammon was the name of the Philistine god (idol) of money. This spirit affects more than just the physical aspects of dealing with money. Understanding that mammon is a spirit behind our interaction with money adds a layer of seriousness to Yeshua's choice of words.

The spirit of mammon is an idol and many people have bowed their knee in worship to it. Mammon controls much of the culture and the decisions that individuals and families make.

Signs of mammon's influence are everywhere. Scripture teaches that we are to give a tenth of our earnings to the storehouse. Although followers of Messiah want to obey G-d, it is in this area of money where testing of faith becomes "real." It is not uncommon for a follower of Messiah to ask the checkbook if it is okay to tithe rather than give the tithe in faith and obedience. The spirit of mammon is at work influencing this decision. The spirit of mammon is also active when one goes to the store to buy a single product and leaves with a basket of items that may or may not be needed. Mammon demands immediate gratification. Another way mammon creeps into our lives is through financial pressure. If we respond in anger or anxiety over a financial pressure rather than in faith and trust, mammon may be influencing our reactions. The spirit of mammon drives the greed and "give to me" nature that many live by. The spirit of mammon is behind much of the anger people feel when financial pressure is on them. The spirit of mammon creates stress and tension through economic pressure.[2]

Yeshua, in His sermon, makes a bold, strong statement, "You cannot serve both G-d and mammon, you will love the one and hate the other." Mammon can become an idol as it is a demonic spirit of destruction. The spirit tempts us to follow it by leading us on an endless chase for material security. This is not new. We see this same spiritual battle take place in the garden of Eden. The serpent tempts Eve with the forbidden fruit by offering her a power and satisfaction that she did not know she wanted. When offered, she could not resist. We fight this same battle today against many spirits and Mammon is one of them. This warfare shows us that we must be submitted to G-d to overcome the temptations.

G-d requires our full devotion.

Deuteronomy 6:4

Love the L-rd your G-d with all your heart, with all your soul and with all your might.

In other words, to love G-d with everything is to value and treasure that which He values and treasures:

Matthew 6:21

For where your treasure is, there will be your heart also.

Deuteronomy 8:11-14 warns Israel to beware of forgetting G-d who delivered them out of Egypt. He warns that when the people have amassed riches they will forget His deliverance and provision.[3]

If my heart is linked to my treasure, then I need to have my heart completely linked to His treasure.

How does this relate to Shabbat? G-d treasures Shabbat so much that He began talking about it in the very first chapter of the Bible. (We will cover this in the next chapter.) To touch the heart of G-d we must pursue what he has treasured in His heart.

This will transform your life and your family. To discover any treasure, we must begin by asking the right question. In this case the right question is, "What does G-d treasure?" The answer is, "Shabbat."

ONE NEW SHABBAT, ONE NEW MAN

The Bible sometimes asks that we obey what we may not understand. But true to His word, He makes Himself known and we grow in our understanding. Shabbat is a gift which when practiced helps us to love the L-rd with all our heart. I am going lay out the Biblical basis for Shabbat. However, even before giving the complete Biblical foundation, we certainly saw in the Isaiah 56 verses 1-2 that G-d treasures the Shabbat and we should treasure that which He values.

Rabbi Shaul uses an olive tree as an analogy to describe the life of the Jew, the Gentile and how faith intersects with one another and G-d. Within this analogy is a curious phrase.

Romans 11:17-18 (ESV)

But if some of the branches were broken off, and you, although a wild olive shoot, were grafted in among the others and now share in the nourishing root of the olive tree, do not be arrogant toward the branches. If you are, remember it is not you who support the root, but the root that supports you.

The nourishing root of the tree is the Hebraic way. The original natural branches were broken off because of unbelief and yet the apostle warns Gentile believers not to be arrogant and standoffish towards them.

Romans 11:19-21

You will say then, "Branches were broken off so that I might be grafted in." True enough. They were broken off because of unbelief, and you stand by faith. Do not be arrogant, but fear—

for if G-d did not spare the natural branches, neither will He spare you.

The roots of the tree are the Hebraic way as laid out in the Torah. The Jewish people are the natural branches that have been cut off due to unbelief in Messiah Yeshua and are grafted back into the tree of life through faith in their promised Jewish Messiah, Yeshua. The Gentile believers are the wild branches that have been grafted into the tree through their faith in the promised Jewish Messiah Yeshua. Both the Jewish people and the Nations will be nourished by the same root, the Biblical Hebraic root.

A few verses earlier, in **Romans 11:11-15**, we read:

I say then, they did not stumble so as to fall, did they? May it never be! But by their false step salvation has come to the Gentiles, to provoke Israel to jealousy. Now if their transgression leads to riches for the world, and their loss riches for the Gentiles, then how much more their fullness! But I am speaking to you who are Gentiles. Insofar as I am an emissary to the Gentiles, I spotlight my ministry if somehow I might provoke to jealousy my own flesh and blood and save some of them. For if their rejection leads to the reconciliation of the world, what will their acceptance be but life from the dead?

Paul teaches us that in the Jewish rejection of Messiah Yeshua, G-d not only continues to offer salvation to the nations, as was previously His pattern, but uses the nations to create a jealous heart in the Jewish people. In verse 15, Paul reminds us: *"If their rejection leads to reconciliation of the world, what will their acceptance be but life from the dead?"*

G-d will not only graft the Jewish people back into the tree of life (olive tree in the analogy) but it is the root of their faith that still nourishes the tree which the rest of the body is grafted. The very root of the tree that brings life to the body and the branches is Hebraic even though most Jews of today are not born-again believers in Messiah Yeshua. This is G-d at his finest: Using those who have been blinded to win the hearts of the world. In winning them, He will eventually win back the hearts of His chosen tribe. I call this "full circle theology."

Gentiles used to usher in the coming of Messiah

Rabbi Yoel Schwartz, head of the Sanhedrin's Noahide Court and of the Dvar Yerushalayim Yeshiva, has written over 200 books and is one of the most respected Haredi (ultra-Orthodox) Jewish leaders in the world. He stated that one of the reasons the Messiah has yet to reveal himself is because the non-Jewish nations are not keeping the Sabbath.

We see the principle explained in an article entitled: SANHEDRIN'S NOAHIDE COURT: MESSIAH REVEALED WHEN NATIONS KEEP THE SABBATH, by Adam Eliyahu Berkowitz, January 10, 2019.

> "We are to teach the nations about *Hashem* (G-d, literally 'the name') and if we do not, the opposite will happen. We will learn idolatry from them, G-d forbid," Rabbi Schwartz told *Breaking Israel News*. "Every Jew knows that the basis of the Torah is the Sabbath. Someone who does not keep the Sabbath, it is as if they are worshiping idols.

> By not instructing the nations in their requirement to 'remember the Sabbath', by preventing them from taking part in the Sabbath, the Jews have prevented the full light of *Moshiach* (Messiah) from being revealed in the world," Rabbi Schwartz said.

> "It is time for a revolution in the world," Rabbi Schwartz said. "Even the secular people who don't believe in G-d know the world is in danger, though they blame it on things like Global Warming. The Sabbath is a precious gift that Hashem gave to the Jews and it demands respect.

But it is time religious Jews showed the nations how they can relate to their Creator."[1]

He called on all the non-Jewish nations to keep the sabbath.

Here is one of the most prominent Jewish leaders in Israel calling on the nations to practice Shabbat. Rabbi Schwartz stated the Torah itself is built around the Shabbat and that by the Jewish people not sharing this with the world, they have prevented the Messiah from being "revealed." His word revealed is very powerful. Like Paul said in Romans 11, as the nations practice faith the Jews will become jealous and then they will see that Yeshua is Messiah. In other words, Yeshua is revealed to the Jews when the nations practice Shabbat.

Followers of Yeshua (Jesus) know that He has come once, and we are awaiting His second coming.

We will see many Jewish people come to faith in Yeshua as Messiah in these last days. That is an event that could usher in the return of Yeshua. Imagine for a moment a bigger vision of Shabbat than just a day off work. Imagine the larger spiritual context of this great day. Imagine your role in the discipleship of the nations and particularly the Jewish nation. Imagine leading the Jewish people to faith in Messiah Yeshua because you begin to guard and keep Shabbat as the Bible teaches. Gentiles who embrace Shabbat are a key to the mystery of the return of Yeshua.

A wonderful truth beckons. As the Jewish people come to faith in Yeshua as the Messiah of Israel and of the nations, we come closer to 'life from the dead" for all people. This power of resurrection comes in part from Gentile believers walking out their faith in a way that makes Jewish people jealous for what they have. This can happen as Gentile believers are being nourished and taught through the Hebraic root. (See Romans chapters 9,10 and 11)

The Bible is a "full circle" concept. G-d brought the law, the covenants, the prophets, the scriptures, and the Messiah through the Jews. The Gentiles received the Messiah, the scriptures, the prophets, covenants, and law. However, the understanding and teaching for the last two thousand years through the Gentile church has been devoid of much that was in the Hebraic root. The time has come for a return to that foundational faith root.

G-d gave the world the Messiah through the Jews and first century Jewish leadership rejected him. Now the world that accepted the Messiah (Gentiles) must return Him to the Jews that they may see and accept Him. Why? Because the way in which He is revealed to the Jews is through the way He lived: Hebraically.

Do you remember the story of Joseph in Genesis Chapters 37-50? Joseph, the 11th son of Jacob was sold by his brothers into slavery when he was seventeen years old. After becoming a great man in the home in which he served he was wrongfully accused of a crime. He spent years in prison with no hope of parole. G-d supernaturally brought him out of his prison, and he was elevated to become the second most powerful person in all of Egypt. Egypt was the world power at the time.

His brothers, who had sold him into slavery decades earlier had to come to Egypt to beg for food during a drought. When they arrived, they were met by Joseph, however, they did not recognize him. Joseph was in Egyptian clothing, spoke Egyptian, and was in the context of a leader of Egypt. It had been decades since they last saw him and his status, garments and language were all blinding for them. They could not recognize their own brother.

Joseph, however, did recognize his brothers. Through the story he tests them and even threatens them.

Genesis 42:8-9

Though Joseph recognized his brothers, they did not recognize him. Then Joseph remembered the dreams he had dreamed about them. He said to them, "You're spies! You've come to see the undefended places in the land."

Finally, when Joseph sees his youngest brother, Benjamin, he breaks down and weeps. The truth is beginning to sink in. Joseph missed his family. He had been treated poorly but yet he longed for his family to be reunited. Joseph loved his father and brothers. I am sure that many of us can relate to this. Even in families that are unhealthy, there is the natural desire for the family to be restored and healthy. Our family is the most important earthly relationship we are given. When divided, our souls are awash with sadness and pain. Restoration of family is the cry of the heart. This was Joseph's cry.

As Joseph pushes one more test he finds it is too much for him to bear:

Genesis 45:1-8

Now Joseph could no longer restrain himself in front of all those who were standing by him, so he cried out, "Get everyone away from me!" So no one stood with him when Joseph made himself known to his brothers. But he gave his voice to weeping so that the Egyptians heard, and Pharaoh's household heard. Joseph said to his brothers, "I am Joseph! Is my father still alive?" And his brothers were unable to answer him because they were terrified at his presence.

Then Joseph said to his brothers, "Please come near me." So they came near. "I'm Joseph, your brother—the one you sold to Egypt," he said. "So now, don't be grieved and don't be angry in your own eyes that you sold me here—since it was for preserving life that God sent me here before you. For there has been two years of famine in the land, and there will be five more years yet with no plowing or harvesting. But God sent me ahead of you to ensure a remnant in the land and to keep you alive for a great escape. So now, it wasn't you, you didn't send me here, but God! And He made me as a father to Pharaoh, lord over his whole house and ruler over the entire land of Egypt.

The power of that moment: The abused, wrongfully treated, and incriminated brother and son is resurrected in front of his family. This incredible scene is prophetic of the day in which the Jewish people will recognize their brother who is also their savior.

During the time of Yeshua, the Jewish leaders in effect sold Yeshua to the nations. The nations accepted Him. The nations that accept Him as Messiah have benefited greatly. They have received incredible blessings from the G-d of Abraham, Isaac, and Jacob. These blessings include forgiveness of sin, eternal life to be granted on the day of judgement, the conscious presence of Adonai in daily life, the gift of the teachings by the Spirit of G-d Himself as promised by the prophets, Ezekiel, Jeremiah, and Joel. These blessings are amazing yet they still lack the fullness of "life from the dead" because the natural born brothers have had Yeshua hidden from them.

For 2000 years, Yeshua, has in many ways been in foreign clothing and speaking with a foreign tongue. Today there is an opportunity to know and worship the King in the way in which he lived.

Yeshua (Jesus) was a Jew in the first century and lived a Hebraic lifestyle including the practice of weekly Shabbat and annual celebration of the feasts of the L-rd. As the Hebraic way of life described in the Bible is restored to the body of Messiah, the Jews will fulfill **Zechariah 12:10** where they will see the *"One whom they pierced"* crying out *"Baruch Haba B'shem Adonai, Blessed is he who comes in the L-rd."*

The prophetic story of Joseph is a picture of what can happen when the nations present Messiah Yeshua to the Jewish people as Jewish rather than in foreign garb and foreign tongue. The practices of the Biblical ways including Shabbat reveal to the Jewish people the glory of salvation. When this happens, prophecy is fulfilled: LIFE FROM THE DEAD!

SHABBAT...I THOUGHT IT WAS JEWISH

As a young boy, my family and I traveled to see my Jewish grandparents in Washington, DC. I do not recall the time of year, but I believe it must have been in December. My grandparents always gave me a piece of *gelt*, which is a chocolate candy wrapped in a gold foil to look like a coin. Traditionally, *gelt* is used at Hanukkah to play dreidel and to satisfy the sweet tooth of young and old. Hanukkah is not the Jewish Christmas, but rather a celebration to remember the deliverance and saving of the Jewish people from the Syrian/Greeks during what is known as the Maccabean revolt around 165 B.C.E. *Gelt* is a symbol of restoration of the temple and the people. I didn't know the history of the Maccabean revolt as a child, but I didn't care as I opened the chocolate to enjoy its rich flavor. This traditional holiday is not commanded in the Bible. It is a wonderful Jewish holiday and like other cultures, Jewish people have many traditions.

The celebration of Christmas, which is a tradition of Christians, marks the celebration of the birth of the Messiah. Like Hanukkah, it is not commanded in the Bible either. Christmas has its own set of celebratory markings from the nativity scene to holiday songs. Although not found in the scriptures, these traditions celebrating the birth of the Messiah, can add meaning in a family celebration.

Traditions can be wonderful, and I certainly enjoy our cultural and family traditions. My rule is simple: If a tradition reinforces the scriptures, then enjoy the tradition, but if the tradition replaces or contradicts the scripture then ditch it. Religious traditions should increase desire for more of the scriptures and encourage study and obedience. A tradition is not bad just because it is not in the Bible, however a tradition must not replace Biblical truth.

Traditions should never be the most important part of a holiday. As much as I enjoy Hanukkah, it does not carry the scriptural significance of the Leviticus 23 appointed times, discussed below. Rather, the Jewish tradition memorializes a great victory in Jewish history. But G-d does not command that we observe Hanukkah any more than He commands observance of Christmas.

The Moadim are not Traditions.

In the scriptures, G-d provided a calendar of events to follow. The Bible speaks of holidays and feasts. All of these are listed in the books of the Torah (the first five books of the Bible). In Leviticus 23 the Torah gives a full listing of the feasts of the L-rd along with instructions on how to celebrate. An appointed time is called a מוֹעֵד "*moed*" in Hebrew. They are appointments that G-d made with mankind to rehearse His story of redemption and return. These feasts are celebrated annually to remind us of G-d's story and our part in it.

Leviticus 23 reveals the significance of Shabbat. Notably, Shabbat is the first appointed time set forth in Leviticus 23.

Leviticus 23:1-4

Then Adonai spoke to Moses saying: "Speak to Bnei-Yisrael, and tell them: These are the appointed moadim of Adonai, which you are to proclaim to be holy convocations—My moadim. Work may be done for six days, but the seventh day is a Shabbat of solemn rest, a holy convocation. You are to do no work—it is a Shabbat to Adonai in all your dwellings. "These are the appointed feasts of Adonai, holy convocations which you are to proclaim in their appointed season.

Shabbat is the first designated time and holy convocation. It is an echo of creation to work six days and take a day of rest on the seventh day, practiced by the first humans before the fall of man. This is G-d's pattern, repeated. Participating in His pattern is fundamentally important.

You can already see that the Biblical calendar is not just annual feasts such as Yom Kippur (Day of Atonement). The weekly Shabbat is included in the regular holiday cycle. The fact that this day is listed in Genesis 2:1-3 and here, as the first appointed time, should indicate to us the great importance G-d has placed on this day. The observance is commanded to happen every seven days, year in and year out, for eternity.

Note a critical distinction: Shabbat is not just a Jewish observance but a Biblical mandate for all humankind. Unfortunately, many people over the last 2000 years have classified a seventh day Shabbat as a Jewish day of worship rather than a Biblical day of worship. Most believers today hear the word Sabbath and equate it to Sunday. Some even propose that you can choose whatever day you want for your Sabbath.

I want you to grasp the magnitude of this idea. Shabbat is from G-d, and as the verse above proclaimed is "for" G-d. As recorded in the scriptures, Shabbat is also for all humankind. Shabbat is a command for ALL people to work six days and on the seventh day rest. Later in the book we will deal with the question, "How do we know that Saturday is the seventh day?" For now, let's just recognize that this holy day is for all people and is on the seventh day.

How Shabbat has kept Israel

Shabbat has been labeled a Jewish celebration because Jews have faithfully observed Shabbat on the seventh day since Biblical times.

Before the Shabbat was given to "am Yisrael" (the People of Israel), it was given to the world. Israel was charged with sharing the gift with others.

For the Jewish people, Shabbat is a sacred weekly event accompanied by many traditions and customs. The power of holding to the Shabbat has been one of the major factors in the solidarity of the Jewish people even as there have been religious divisions. After not having a homeland, a civil government, a temple, or local community to call their own for over two thousand years, the Jewish people seemed to be in step with one another and their faith when they were granted the State of Israel in 1948. The power of keeping Shabbat throughout the diaspora was a significant reason they had a common unity. In fact, there is an ancient Jewish saying, that underscores how deeply Shabbat resides in Jewish hearts: "More than Israel has kept Shabbat, Shabbat has kept Israel."[1]

Let us go back in time for a moment. Look up, imagine seeing the night sky with no stars. Imagine seeing only darkness, no lights of any kind. In that moment in time, G-d spoke and created day one. The earth was formless and void. There was a presence in the universe, darkness. This presence felt heavy and evil. There has been a war in the heavenly realm. A strong being, referred to as the serpent (*nāḥāš* נָחָשׁ) has gathered a third of the other angels to his war cry. They had been in one accord in fellowship with the One true G-d until the serpent persuaded them to leave the glory of the L-rd and follow him. He convinced them that he was a greater ruler than the one who created them. In their deception they attempted a coup. It was short lived, and almost as quickly as the attack ensued it was over. The creator of all the universe, of all power, of all energy simply removed the threat by casting the serpent from His presence. The fall looked like lightening striking into this realm we call earth (Luke 10:18, Isaiah 14:12-15, Revelation 12:1-8). At the time of the fall, earth was dark, formless, and void. In the darkness, a presence now exists, and it was evil.

The Creator had a plan of redemption and releases it by saying, Genesis 1:2 *"Let there be Light."*

With that, G-d gave a piece of Himself as light into the realm He would soon fill with mankind. With this light came an organized energy forming the earth. He separated light from darkness. The serpent was condemned to the darkness and given several titles (including the Satan/accuser, the devil, the dragon, the enemy), until such time of his final judgement and destruction when he will be banished to eternal darkness. (Separation from the Creator)

Creation sets off a clock.

And so it began:

Genesis 1:5

God called the light "day," and the darkness He called "night." So there was evening and there was morning—one day.

During the next five days, G-d is in creation mode. He is using His imagination and building a universe full of stars, suns, moons, and planets. When he creates our planet it is full of complexity, life, and beauty. At the end of each day He looks at His work and states how good it is. These days of creation can be seen as a way in which G-d organizes all that exists. The first three days are building the structures: the heavens, the stars, the lights, the earth, the seas, etc. The next three days He works from the top down and fills the structures with life: birds to the air, fish to the seas and animals to the land. With day six, He creates a living being in His image. Each day of creation builds upon the previous day adding layers of intricacy and when He is finished, he caps off the masterful work week with proclaiming all good, and He RESTS.

What is the most important day of creation week?

Is the seventh day less valuable in the sight of G-d than the sixth day? When we consider how important each of the other days of creation is to G-d and most certainly to us, would it be right to say the seventh day was not of the same value? If that were the case, then why even mention the seventh day. Why not just finish on the sixth day--with giving us life--and say, "It is good?" He could have chosen to simply move on with the narrative. However, He did not. We are told the following:

Genesis 2:1-3

Thus the heavens and the earth were finished, along with everything in them. On the seventh day G-d was finished with his work which he had made, so he rested on the seventh day from all his work which he had made. G-d blessed the seventh day and separated it as holy; because on that day G-d rested from all his work which he had created, so that it itself could produce. (CJB)

Not only are we told there is a seventh day, but we are told that G-d rested, blessed it, and separated it as a holy day. Think about this for a moment. Can you or I do what G-d did the first six days? NO! We can never create life like G-d. We can recreate, we can discover, we can partner with G-d, and we can be a part of the process of creation, but G-d alone deserves the title of original creator. But the seventh day, the Shabbat, is the day that G-d leaves as an invitation to us to be in fellowship with Him. This day, the Shabbat, we can do as G-d did and rest.

I remember hearing sports caster Bob Costas answer a question about why he loved golf so much. He told a story of how one day on the famed par 3 of Pebble Beach he hit a shot that landed within an inch of being a hole-in-one. On that day, at that moment, the greatest golf players in the world, Palmer, Nicholas, Woods could not have made a better shot. Costas said that golf is the only sport where the average guy at any given moment can be as great as the greatest player in the world.

Shabbat is one thing G-d did and told us to do just like Him. We are invited to fellowship with Him and imitate Him on the seventh day.

The creation story of Genesis sets the precedent that Shabbat is not based on the laws given at Sinai through Moses, but rather from the very beginning of all that has ever been done in the universe. At Sinai, He confirmed that Shabbat was commanded. The fourth commandment tells us to, *"Remember the Sabbath and keep it holy."* In other words, G-d is calling us to follow His example. WOW. Six days you work, but on the seventh day do what G-d does and REST.

Shabbat is a foundation of creation and built into the fabric of our existence and interaction with G-d. If it is important enough to include in the creation narrative, then certainly we are wise to consider its importance in our lives.

Shabbat is the day set apart by G-d as a treasure to those who would follow His ways. Yeshua reminds us in Matthew 6:21 that, *"Where your treasure is there your heart will be also."* G-d treasures the seventh day as much as the other six days. In fact, it could be argued that G-d treasures the seventh day more than the other days considering He separated the seventh day and called it alone a holy day. This is the only day of creation that He defined for us. The other six days are workdays, and we are commanded to work, but on the seventh we must do as G-d does and rest.

A Warning about Assumptions

Over the centuries we have seen churches offer different interpretations and applications of Shabbat. Many times, the teachings of the Hebrew scriptures (Old Testament) are consciously or subconsciously put in the category of either a moral principle or a replaced law. In general, it has become normal practice to only accept teachings of the New Testament. For example, law and grace are considered by many to be opposing ideas. Shabbat also has fallen into this category. Many of you reading this may carry some general assumptions that put a wall of separation up between you and the plain teaching of scripture. I want to encourage you to ask G-d right now to remove all assumptions you have about Shabbat, the Old Testament and following the commands that come from those scriptures. Let us allow the Bible to speak for itself and give us the truth.

Come with me to explore the spiritual foundation which must be understood to comprehend the power of Shabbat.

Law and Grace:

Laws given in the Bible are commandments to be obeyed (Note: all laws of the Hebrew Bible are not still in practice although the principles may be active, such as laws concerning the temple). When the law is broken, we know this as sin. A sinner is a law breaker and Romans 3:23 confirms that *"all have sinned and fall short of the glory of G-d."* When the law is broken there is a cost for that sin. The lawbreaker is required to pay a penalty.

The scriptures teach there will be an afterlife. A soul will gain immortality or suffer destruction.

Isaiah 26:19

Your dead shall live; their bodies shall rise. You who dwell in the dust, awake and sing for joy! For your dew is a dew of light, and the earth will give birth to the dead.

G-d says "your" dead referring to the dead who are in His hand and will rise again.

Daniel 12:2 makes it clearer:

And many of those who sleep in the dust of the earth shall awake, some to everlasting life, and some to shame and everlasting contempt.

Psalm 16:10 tells us about who G-d saves:

For you will not abandon my soul to Sheol, or let your holy one see corruption.

Holiness is attained either by our own works, which always falls short or by receiving forgiveness for the failures. How do we attain this forgiveness? The Torah lays it out clearly.

Leviticus 17:11

For the life of the flesh is in the blood, and I have given it for you on the altar to make atonement for your souls, for it is the blood that makes atonement by the life.

Hebrews 9:22 reiterates this:

Indeed, under the law almost everything is purified with blood, and without the shedding of blood there is no forgiveness of sins.

So, if we are to walk out holiness and righteousness, we must realize that we are going to need forgiveness. Each time we break the law of G-d we sin. It is blood that atones for our transgression. This atonement grants us the gift of immortality to live in eternity in the presence of G-d.

Ultimately, the penalty of being lawless will happen in the next life, when the lawbreaker faces the judgement seat of the L-rd and will be asked to give a reckoning for the laws that have been broken. For the believer in Messiah Yeshua who has been born again, the answer will simply be given from Messiah himself. He will state that the lawbreaker is guilty of sin but that He, Messiah, has taken the penalty for him and therefore the justice required is completed. There are no longer sins on the ledger of the sinner. The judge will then proclaim "not guilty" for the lawbreaker. The blessing for being not guilty is Eternal Life. That's right: G-d is going to grant eternal life to all those who are found not guilty.

However, for those who do not believe in the Messiah Yeshua and claim they can handle their own life, the outcome will be quite different. When asked about bearing the burden of guilt associated with being a lawbreaker, the ones without faith in Messiah will themselves have to pay the penalty for their crimes.. Why? Remember, Leviticus 17:11 says: *"For the life of the flesh is in the blood, and I have given it for you on the altar to make atonement for your souls, for it is the blood that makes atonement by the life."*

Blood is required for the atonement of sin and anyone without the prescribed and acceptable sacrifice from G-d, Yeshua, will have to pay the penalty for his or her own sin, eternal death.

However, one may ask if sin is to be forgiven at the judgement day, and we have no eternal punishment awaiting, can't we just keep breaking the laws of G-d and get forgiveness later? This question has been asked numerous times over the centuries. If someone wants to keep sinning after declaring and receiving Yeshua as L-rd then it is possible they have only become born into an intellectual knowledge of Messiah. For one who has a heart transformation through faith, the desire to keep sinning loses its grip.

Nonetheless, transformed, born-again believers still sin. Many times we even pay a price for them here on earth. For example, the eighth commandment states that to lie is a sin. Ultimately if I live my life as a liar and have no redemption from the blood atonement of Yeshua, then I will end up with eternal death for that sin. However, if I am born again and I lie, I may still ruin relationships here on earth with people as I break trust. The difference is that I will repent here because I have a relationship with my heavenly father, and He will convict me of my sin. I will submit to Him and be changed. In addition, even though I lied on earth, due to grace and my real relationship with the Father through the Son, I will be granted immunity and given the gift of eternal life.

Understand this cycle: We are separated from G-d by our sin and can receive forgiveness from and restoration to our G-d only through faith in His Son, Yeshua (Jesus) and His atoning sacrifice, giving us hope now for the future.

What does this have to do with Shabbat?

I have watched as people who become convicted about the practice of Shabbat, walk in regret, and even ungodly condemnation about their past. I have seen people begin to doubt their own experiences with G-d when they learn that the Sabbath which they were taught about is not the Shabbat of the Bible. I wanted you to be aware that G-d is loving, forgiving and works in many ways. I am born-again because G-d used the protestant church practice to lead me to the Son. My upbringing, my faith experiences, are no less valuable and were not sin to me. G-d has chosen to reveal Shabbat to me and this does not negate that He used another method to bring me into His kingdom. As G-d reveals Shabbat to you, remember that the new revelation is for you to grow and move forward with G-d rather than to disdain the past revelation.

Shabbat is not a Jewish religious practice but rather a treasured gift from G-d intended for you to enjoy. Shabbat is an invitation to ALL peoples to enter into fellowship with the creator of the Universe.

Jeff Friedlander

Five Boundaries of Shabbat

I ended the last chapter with a serious call to obedience of G-d's commands. I also hope I made it clear that obeying the law of G-d will never make you righteous or born again. Your heavenly calling and born-again status is only secured by faith in Messiah Yeshua as the Savior and substitute for your penalty of sin.

Ephesians 2:8-9

For by grace you have been saved through faith. And this is not your own doing; it is the gift of G-d, not a result of works, so that no one may boast.

It is our faith and not our works that saves us. We are only sure of our salvation because of our faith in the finished work of the Messiah. We are filled with the Holy Spirit and demonstrate our faith through works. Faith is an action not just a belief.

So, when it comes to Shabbat people ask "Is it a command?" "Am I obligated to obey?" Let's look at the scriptures for answers.

Five characteristics or commands of Shabbat

Genesis 2:1-3

*So, the heavens and the earth were completed along with their entire array. G-d completed—**on the seventh day**—His work that He made, and **He ceased—on the seventh day**—from all His work that He made. Then **G-d blessed** the seventh day and **sanctified it**, for on it He ceased from all His work that G-d created for the purpose of preparing.*

Deuteronomy 5: 12-15

'Observe Yom Shabbat to **keep it holy**, as Adonai your G-d commanded you. **Six days you are to labor** and do all your work, but the seventh day is a Shabbat to Adonai your G-d. In it you are not to do any work—not you or your son or your daughter, or your slave or your maid, or your ox, your donkey or any of your livestock or the outsider within your gates, so that your slave and your maid may rest as you do. You must remember that you were a slave in the land of Egypt, and Adonai your G-d brought you out from there with a mighty hand and an outstretched arm. Therefore, Adonai your G-d commanded you to keep Yom Shabbat.

Exodus 20:8-11

"Remember Yom Shabbat, to keep it holy. You are to work six days, and do all your work, but the seventh day is a Shabbat to Adonai your G-d. In it you shall not do any work—not you, nor your son, your daughter, your male servant, your female servant, your cattle, nor the outsider that is within your gates. For in six days Adonai made heaven and earth, the sea, and all that is in them, and rested on the seventh day. Thus, Adonai blessed Yom Shabbat, and made it holy. It is a day of rest from work for people and animals.

In these verses, we see some key obligations regarding Shabbat. I have listed several other supporting verses in the Bible for each point.

1. Work is to be done for the first six days of the week.

See also: Exodus 20:9, 31:15, 34:21, 35:2 Leviticus 23:3, Luke 13:14, Ezekiel 46:1

This powerful truth is the foundation for how we are to structure our lives. The sacredness of Shabbat encompasses many aspects of our lives. A foundational element is the weekly recognition of our dependence on G-d. Our weekly work tempts us to believe the work of our hands is our primary provision, however when we take one day to cease from work and put our trust in the pattern of G-d, we reset our minds to be centered on G-d. We take time to recognize that G-d's ways are higher than our ways and His thoughts are higher than our thoughts. We fall in line with Isaiah 55:9 and following verses. There is a supernatural reset of priorities.

The founding fathers of America demonstrated this dependence in their writings. Again and again, we read in their personal letters, speeches, and legal papers the phrase, "due to providence," "because of Your providence," etc. This providence was understood to be the G-d of the Bible which included the Tanakh (Old Testament) and the New Testament (Apostolic Letters). They were convinced that no matter how hard they fought, how good they were, or how much they tried to be better than their enemies, G-d's providential work on their behalf would be the reason they would succeed.

Benjamin Franklin, who some claim was a deist, had this to say at the constitutional convention:

> "I have lived, Sir, a long time, and the longer I live, the more convincing proofs I see of this truth – that G-d governs in the affairs of men. And if a sparrow cannot fall to the ground without his notice, is it probable that an empire can rise without his aid?"[1]

Clearly this man believed that G-d has providence as He watches over the sparrow and this providence carries forward to the rise of an empire.

This is a good time for a heart check. Is our work successful because of our efforts or because G-d has provided the labor and the skill? With this thought in mind we come to Shabbat each week to be reminded of the providence of heaven. By removing ourselves from our labor we can pause and reflect on what He has done for us.

2. Shabbat is the seventh day of the week.

Genesis 2:2 Exodus 20:10, 16:26, 31:17, Leviticus 23:3, Deuteronomy 5:14

Why would the day of the week matter? In a later chapter we will deal with this in greater detail, but for now, consider this: Is it okay to ask G-d a question? Yes, it is perfectly acceptable, permissible, and even desirable for us to ask G-d questions. However, it is never acceptable to question G-d. Many look at a command that Shabbat is on the seventh day and rather than accept it as the word of G-d, they question His choice of the seventh day. They justify this line of questioning by speaking for G-d and saying "Would G-d really care on which day of the week we take a Shabbat?" Many have gone so far as to assign Shabbat to the day of their personal choosing.

The result is that we answered the question we have asked. For the last 2000 years, the answer we've given ourselves has been, "We don't agree that He defines the day of the week for rest and so we justify our choosing of the day we desire." Theoretically, under this rationale, we could choose a different day each week since we have now determined it is up to us anyway.

G-d said the seventh day is the Shabbat. That should be enough.

3. Shabbat is to be kept holy.

Deuteronomy 5:12, Genesis 2:1-3, Isaiah 58:13-14, Exodus 31:14, 20:11

An earmark of the people who follow the G-d of the Bible is that their actions and ways are different from other groups or cultures. We are a people who are set apart. The Hebrew word for set apart is "kadosh" (קָדוֹשׁ) which translates as HOLY. Shabbat is set apart from the other six days. Another word we could use to describe this time is 'sacred.' Later in this book, we will look more in depth at the sacred aspects of Shabbat. Sacredness distinguishes this day from all others. There is an intangible quality to this day and when the light of holiness shines on Shabbat we begin to see how different it is from the other days of the week.

4. Shabbat is a day of rest.

In addition to the scriptures above, see also Genesis 2:1-3, Exodus 20:9-10, 20:11, 31:14-15, 34:21, 35:2, Leviticus 23:3, Luke 13:14, Ezekiel 16:26, 31:17, 46:1, Deuteronomy 5:12-14, Isaiah 55:9, 58:13-14

As you are seeing in this book, rest is a central theme of Shabbat. When one properly understands how G-d designed us then one can appreciate rest, and will desire it every week. It will become an integral part of your life.

5. Shabbat is a commemoration of creation.

Exodus 20:11

Shabbat is a good time to weekly marvel at the creation that surrounds us. Meditate on the wonders that G-d has done in your life over the previous week. As you begin to engage the creator who thoughtfully created this world we live in, it will humble you to recognize that this G-d set aside one day a week to make an appointment of rest with you. Reflecting on His power to create will astonish and inspire. Shabbat provides the opportunity to pause and reflect on the creator of our soul; the other six days of the work week do not allow this contemplative experience.

Are there some other commands surrounding the Shabbat? Yes. For example, **Isaiah 58:13-14** says:

If you turn back your foot from Shabbat, from doing your pleasure on My holy day, and call Shabbat a delight, the holy day of Adonai honorable, If you honor it, not going your own ways, not seeking your own pleasure, nor speaking your usual speech, then You will delight yourself in Adonai, and I will let you ride over the heights of the earth, I will feed you with the heritage of your father Jacob. For the mouth of Adonai has spoken.

What does "not going your own ways, not seeking your own pleasure, nor speaking your usual speech" mean? These are part of Shabbat but too many religious leaders have tried to tell people legalistically exactly what is meant. I will not tell you what to do but I will be giving you Biblical boundaries.

For example, consider **Exodus 35:3**.

Do not kindle a fire in any of your dwellings on Yom Shabbat.

There have been large volumes of work produced on what this verse means. Although kindling a fire is prohibited on Shabbat, we must find what that means from G-d's perspective rather than our own. (Later on, I will give some definition for you to consider about what not kindling a fire means.)

There are some big issues when it comes to obeying Shabbat but one principle that should always be employed is the principle of HEART. G-d prioritizes the heart of a person above all else. Where the heart goes, the behavior and actions will follow. So, if your heart is to keep and guard Shabbat as commanded, then over time G-d will give you the practical application of that desire.

What are the requirements we are to meet to truly obey G-d's command to keep the Shabbat? As we go through the rest of this book you will learn the commands of G-d about Shabbat and practical ways you can obey G-d.

HOW YESHUA KEPT SHABBAT?

Many years ago, the WWJD craze hit the Christian scene. People wore bracelets and t-shirts asking, "What Would Jesus Do (WWJD)?" We can ask that question about the practice of Shabbat: "WWJD?"

Let's look at the scriptures.

John 1:1-5

In the beginning was the Word. The Word was with G-d, and the Word was G-d. He was with G-d in the beginning. All things were made through Him, and apart from Him nothing was made that has come into being. In Him was life, and the life was the light of men. The light shines in the darkness, and the darkness has not overpowered it.

The "Word" is referring to the person of Yeshua. This is a foundational truth. The "Word" was G-d, and was with G-d in the beginning. This is a clue to the answer to our question.

Remember in Genesis 2:1-3, G-d rested on the seventh day. If the word is Yeshua and the Word is G-d and was with G-d in the beginning, then we can conclude that Yeshua practiced the very first Shabbat after creation. In a sense then, Yeshua instituted Shabbat.

What about His incarnation on the earth? Did he practice Shabbat while on the earth?

We have already established that Shabbat is a command. Yeshua lived a sinless life to become the sacrificial offering for our atonement. **1 Peter 2:22** tells us that, *"He committed no sin, and* *no deceit was found in his mouth."* It follows that of course Yeshua kept Shabbat as commanded by the scriptures.

Luke 4:16-30

Yeshua returned in the power of the Ruach to the Galilee, and news about Him went out through all the surrounding region. He taught in their synagogues, and everyone was praising Him. And He came to Natzeret, where He had been raised. As was His custom, He went into the synagogue on Shabbat, and He got up to read. When the scroll of the prophet Isaiah was handed to Him, He unrolled the scroll and found the place where it was written, "The Ruach Adonai is on me, because He has anointed me to proclaim Good News to the poor. He has sent me to proclaim release to the captives and recovery of sight to the blind, to set free the oppressed, and to proclaim the year of Adonai's favor." He closed the scroll, gave it back to the attendant, and sat down. All eyes in the synagogue were focused on Him. Then He began to tell them, "Today this Scripture has been fulfilled in your ears."

The common practice of the first century was to gather in the synagogue on the Shabbat to read the scriptures, study, and worship. Yeshua followed the customs of the day as evidenced in verse 16. He went to the synagogue on Shabbat in Naz'ret and read the scriptures. This particular reading was from Isaiah 61 and Yeshua revealed his identity, as the promised and prophesied Jewish Messiah.

As we continue to follow the footsteps of Yeshua, the next verses take us to Capernaum where again Yeshua goes to the synagogue on Shabbat to teach. This is a powerful story of how Yeshua practices Shabbat. He not only follows the customs but reveals the heart of Shabbat by healing a demon possessed man.

Luke 4:31-37

Yeshua came down to Capernaum, a town in the Galilee. He was teaching them on Shabbat, and they were astounded at His teaching because His message had authority. In the synagogue was a man who had an unclean demonic spirit, and he cried out with a loud voice, "Ah! What have we to do with You, Yeshua of Natzeret? Have You come to destroy us? I know who You are! You are the Holy One of G-d!"

Yeshua rebuked him, saying, "Quiet! Come out of him!" And when the demon threw him down in their midst, it came out without hurting him.

They were all amazed, and they spoke to one another, saying, "What is this message? For with authority and power He commands the unclean spirits, and they come out." So His reputation grew, spreading to every place in that region.

This is a very important point for those who have been wanting to practice their faith the way Yeshua practiced his faith. There are four gospel accounts written about Yeshua and in each of them He is seen going to synagogue on Shabbat--teaching, healing, and blessing. Given that the Pharisees imposed many Shabbat customs and rules on the people, they often confronted Yeshua about his Shabbat practice.

These encounters give us a clue as to how G-d defines Shabbat. Let's look at **Luke 13:10-17** to see how Yeshua responds to the Pharisees when confronted about healing Shabbat.

Now Yeshua was teaching in one of the synagogues on Shabbat. And behold, there was a woman with a disabling spirit for eighteen years, bent over and completely unable to stand up straight. When Yeshua saw her, He called out to her and said, "Woman, you are set free from your disability." Then He laid hands on her, and instantly she stood up straight and began praising G-d.

But the synagogue leader, indignant that Yeshua had healed on Shabbat, started telling the crowd, "There are six days in which work should be done—so come to be healed on those days and not on Yom Shabbat!"

But the L-rd answered him and said, "Hypocrites! On Shabbat doesn't each of you untie his ox or donkey from the stall and lead it away to give it drink? So this one, a daughter of Abraham incapacitated by Satan for eighteen years, shouldn't she be set free from this imprisonment on Yom Shabbat?" When Yeshua said these things, all His opponents were put to shame; but the whole crowd was rejoicing at all the glorious things done by Him.

Yeshua clearly addresses the false teaching that it is not permissible to heal on Shabbat.

We see that Yeshua honored the Shabbat and some of the practices of the day, but He did not endorse false teaching, customs or rules that were against Torah. In addition, he NEVER changed the day of Shabbat from the seventh day to another day. He had many teaching opportunities to make this change, but He did not.

The conclusion is obvious. Yeshua practiced the Shabbat in obedience to the commands of scripture and in alignment with the customs of his people.

PAST AND NEXT GENERATIONS

One of my greatest joys in life is watching my kids grow and change. Today I am blessed with four accomplished young adult children. When they were little children, I enjoyed observing them discover and marvel over the mysteries of the world around them. As they grew older the inevitable questions were asked..." Who am I? What is my purpose? Does G-d know me, and do I know Him?" My wife and I endeavored to live our faith authentically. We wanted to be an example before our children. Our desire was to raise our children in the admonition and knowledge of G-d. We knew at some point that each child would have to individually receive the revelation of the Messiah for themselves.

This Biblical pattern of generational transfer is found in

Psalm 78:4

We will not hide them (the ways of G-d) from their children, telling to the next generation the praises of ADONAI and His strength and the wonders He has done.

Passing faith to the next generation is one of the most important responsibilities of the faithful. I have often said that one of the saddest scriptures in the Bible is **Judges 2:10**. *And all that generation also were gathered to their fathers. And there arose another generation after them who did not know the L-rd or the work that he had done for Israel. (ESV)*

Joshua and his generation did not pass on all that G-d had done for them, therefore their children did not carry out the faith. One vehicle societies use to pass on beliefs is traditions. In Judaism, there are many traditions that teach the faith. Some of these traditions have lasted for thousands of years and are taken directly from scripture. Some are additions to scripture and have created great divisions among Jewish people. Some of those divisions have also kept many Jewish people away from larger society.

One of the traditions of religious observant Jewish people is to repeat a prayer from the Torah each day. This is a great tradition that reinforces the Bible.

This tradition aids in fulfilling generational transfer. In the reciting of the *Shema* prayer, twice a day, (morning, and evening,) as a central prayer of faith, Jewish people are unified around the world.

The Hebrew word *Shema* (שְׁמַע) means "hear or listen." In addition to hearing, *shema* also means obey. Every time you read in the Bible "obey" you are reading a form of the word *shema*. To hear G-d is to obey G-d. In Hebraic thought, listening to G-d cannot be separated from doing what G-d said. We become what we listen to, which is why we must listen to the Word of G-d. As we hear Him speak, we will become obedient to His word and be the people we are designed to be.

The *Shema* comes from:

Deuteronomy 6:4-9

"Hear O Israel, the Lord our God, the Lord is one. Love Adonai your God with all your heart and with all your soul and with all your strength. These words, which I am commanding you today, are to be on your heart. You are to teach them diligently to your children, and speak of them when you sit in your house, when you walk by the way, when you lie down and when you rise up. Bind them as a sign on your hand, they are to be as frontlets between your eyes, and write them on the doorposts of your house and on your gates.

This is the command of G-d. We are to teach our children diligently. More than the words of these verses, we are to teach them the word of G-d. The Torah, the prophets, the writings, the covenants, the commands, the brit hadasha (New Testament or covenant), the heart of our Father in heaven and how to be in relationship with Him and others. The *Shema* is prayed in the morning and the evening each day and has been one of the most influential traditions in Jewish history. The verse "When you rise up and when you go to sleep" is interpreted to mean we are to say this prayer twice a day. This is a Hebrew idiom: Evening and Morning are an indication of the fullness of each day and the continuation of each day we are to practice "teaching our children" the commands of G-d. The bigger idea is that we are to always look for ways to pass the teachings of G-d to the next generation.

We cannot underestimate the power of this idea. Imagine what society would be like today if we took seriously the command to have as our highest priority, night and day, our faith being practiced and taught to our children.

The *Shema* is summarized in a few sentences for easy memory and recitation. Be encouraged to incorporate this into your daily walk of faith. In addition to Deuteronomy 6:4, the *Shema* combines parts of Deuteronomy 11 and Numbers 15.

שְׁמַע יִשְׂרָאֵל יְהֹוָה אֱלֹהֵינוּ יְהֹוָה אֶחָד

בָּרוּךְ שֵׁם כְּבוֹד מַלְכוּתוֹ לְעוֹלָם וָעֶד

Sh'ma Yisra'el, Adonai Elohaynoo, Adonai ekhad.

Barookh shem k'vod malkhooto l'olam va'ed.

Hear O Israel, the L-rd our G-d, the L-rd is one. Blessed be His glorious name, whose kingdom is forever and ever.

The Shema is followed by the V'hafta in the evening and morning prayer. This is the rest of the passage Deuteronomy 6:5-9 stated above.

We are the caretakers of the scriptures and thus we must pass on what we have learned to the next generation.

Another of the practices of the faith which we pass on to our children is Shabbat. My wife, Sherri, and I have practiced Shabbat with our children, teaching and modeling to them the blessing of this gift. Today, they all love and long for the Shabbat each week. Their lives have been enriched because we taught them to *shema* (hear) the word of G-d and do as He instructs.

Yeshua modeled this generational transfer with the disciples. Rabbi Shaul (Paul) practiced Shabbat after the resurrection of the Messiah. Shabbat had been his practice; faith in the Messiah did not replace the command of Shabbat.

First Century Discipleship through Shabbat

Acts 17:1-4

After passing through Amphipolis and Apollonia, they came to Thessalonica, where there was a Jewish synagogue. As was his custom, Paul went to the Jewish people; and for three Shabbatot, he debated the Scriptures with them. He opened them and gave evidence that Messiah had to suffer and rise from the dead, saying, "This Yeshua, whom I declare to you, is the Messiah." Some of them were convinced and became attached to Paul and Silas, as were a large number of the G-d-fearing Greeks and no small number of the leading women.

Not only did the Apostle Paul go to the synagogue but specifically, that was his custom. He talked and debated about Messiah and the scriptures. It is worthy to note that verse 4 reveals there were many G-d fearing Greeks and no small number of leading women among those gathered for Shabbat. This lets us see that non-Jews and women were among the audience in the synagogue learning G-d's ways.

The Greek word used to describe these Greeks is **σεβομένων** or *sebomenōn*. This word literally means "worshipping." The

Greeks in attendance had a deep affection for the G-d of Abraham, Isaac, and Jacob.

Also, the makeup of the synagogue included Jews, Greeks, men, and women. This mixture is noted in multiple passages. The New Testament provides a window into the makeup of the first century synagogue. One note of special interest and surprise to some is the substantial number of women who are thought of as leaders throughout the New Testament: Philip's daughters (Acts 21:9), Priscilla (Acts 18:26; Rom. 16:3-5, etc.), Phoebe (Rom. 16:1-2), Junia (Rom. 16:7), possibly Chloe (1 Cor. 1:11), Euodia and Syntyche (Phil. 4:2-3), Nympha (Col. 4:15), Apphia (Phlm. 2), "the chosen lady" (2 John 1), "the chosen sister" (2 John 13), and probably Lydia (Acts 16:40).

The references to attending synagogue on Shabbat throughout the New Testament writings show that the pattern of "keeping the Shabbat" was not broken after the resurrection of Messiah. We are reading events that are happening many years after the resurrection of Yeshua and seeing the Biblical evidence that the practice of the first century believers is to attend the synagogue on Shabbat. Paul made it his practice to visit the synagogues on Shabbat in the towns where he ministered. We don't see the change to Sunday worship until a post-Biblical period.

The idea that "church" and Sunday Sabbath were born **during** the first century is not true.

Here is another travel record of Paul's journey and ministry practice:

Acts 13:13-15

Setting sail from Paphos, Paul's company came to Perga in Pamphylia. John left them and returned to Jerusalem. But they passed on from Perga and came to Antioch of Pisidia. Entering the synagogue on the Shabbat, they sat down. After the reading of the Torah and the Prophets, the synagogue leaders sent to them, saying, "Brothers, if you have any word of encouragement for the people, speak."

Again, we see the company of Paul entering the synagogue on Shabbat. As a Pharisee, it was Paul's practice to be in the synagogue on the seventh day for Shabbat. He continued to do this following the model Yeshua routinely lived out before the disciples. Clearly, the way of reading the Torah and the Prophets on Shabbat did not change with Yeshua but expanded and included non-Jews.

Paul preaches to them and at the end of the message the following happens:

Acts 13:42-44

As Paul and Barnabas were going out, the people kept begging them to speak these things to them the next Shabbat. When the synagogue meeting broke up, many of the Jewish people and G-d-fearing inquirers followed Paul and Barnabas, who were speaking with them and trying to persuade them to continue in the grace of G-d. The following Shabbat, almost the entire city came together to hear the word of the L-rd.

What a testimony! In two Shabbats, G-d reached a city. May it be so in our day!

Of a subsequent journey, we read:

Acts 18:1-4

*After these things, Paul left Athens and went to Corinth. There he found a Jewish man named Aquila—a native of Pontus having recently come from Italy with his wife Priscilla, because Claudius had commanded all Jewish people to leave Rome. Paul went to see them; and because he was of the same trade, he stayed with them and began working, for by trade they were tent-makers. And he was **debating every Shabbat in the synagogue, trying to persuade both Jewish and Greek people.***

Here again we get a glimpse into first century Shabbat. Paul is in the synagogue debating and trying to persuade both Jews and Greeks in the words of Torah and the fulfillment of the Messiah.

What are Paul and his companions doing? Debating and witnessing for Messiah. Who is there? Again, Jews and Greeks. Many come to faith here. The first century synagogue meeting was not like our meetings today. They included elements we include, but the form was much different. As you read through the Bible and see how Yeshua and the apostles acted in the weekly Shabbat meeting you see a pattern. They read the Torah and prophets openly. There would be some teaching by one of the pharisees or leaders. There would be discussion (debate) about the meaning of the passages. There would be words of encouragement given. There would be music and song as well as liturgies. These Shabbat meetings were all participatory meetings rather than places where people watched and observed. The weekly Shabbat gathering was not like attending the theater. They were not gathering to be entertained but rather to engage the scriptures with each other and allow G-d to change them. We (Be One Fellowship) practice this way in our weekly Shabbat gatherings in our homes. (See appendix A for a guide)

We know from history that Paul wrote several letters. Two of these found in the New Testament are to the believers in Corinth, written after his departure from the area. These letters express continuing interaction and discipleship even after Paul spent a year and half in Corinth.

Acts 18:7-11

After leaving there, Paul went into the house of a man named Titus Justus, a G-d-fearer whose house was next door to the synagogue. Crispus, the synagogue leader, put his faith in the L-rd, along with his whole household. And many of the Corinthians, upon hearing, were believing and being immersed.

Now the L-rd said to Paul through a vision in the night, "Do not be afraid, but speak and do not be silent! For I am with you and no one shall attack you to harm you—many people in this city are for Me." So he stayed a year and six months, teaching the word of G-d among them.

We can deduce that Rabbi Shaul engaged in 74 Sabbaths in Corinth, plus the other Shabbats mentioned in Acts. In sum, Paul attended at least 80 Shabbats after Yeshua's death and resurrection.

This was the pattern of the Jewish followers of Messiah and was also the pattern of the Gentiles who came to faith. We know this from reading Acts 15. Although there are many important topics to be discussed from Acts 15 we will only note one:

Acts 15:19-21

*Therefore, I judge not to trouble those from among the Gentiles who are turning to G-d—but to write to them to abstain from the contamination of idols, and from sexual immorality, and from what is strangled, and from blood. For Moses from ancient generations has had in every city those who proclaim him, **since he is read in all the synagogues every Shabbat.** "*

This discussion took place around 50 C.E. The leaders agreed that the new Gentile believers needed to be discipled in the ways of Torah.

In the first century, part of the discipleship plan was to go to synagogue on Shabbat and learn Torah. Moses was read for generations and is still read to this day. Moses was taught in the synagogue to those in attendance. This was the way the Jerusalem council expected the new Gentile believers to learn and grow in the L-rd. The Jerusalem council knew the new non-Jewish believers would need the foundational teaching of the Torah for their growth in their faith in Messiah. The Torah would teach them how to live after being born again.

The Shabbat is on the seventh day of the week. During the writing of the New Testament the Shabbat never changed from the seventh day and the practice of Shabbat was what Paul was teaching the Gentiles. The Jerusalem council affirms the Gentiles would learn of the Bible through coming to Shabbat on the seventh day as had been done for generations.

Post Biblical Records

Many historians, church history experts, and commentators throughout history provide evidence of the keeping of the Shabbat on the seventh day for hundreds of years after resurrection. Here is a small sampling:

"The primitive Christians did keep the Sabbath of the Jews. Therefore, the Christians for a long time together, did keep their conventions on the Sabbath, in which some portion of the Law were read: and this continued till the time of the Laodicean council."[7]

This Laodicean council was held in 363-364 CE. So according to this source, Shabbat on the seventh day, with the tradition of reading from the Torah, was still in practice 300 plus years after Messiah.

"The ancient Christians were very careful in the observation of **Saturday, or the seventh day**. It is plain that all the Oriental churches, and the greatest part of the world, observed the Sabbath as a festival...Athanasius likewise tells us that they held religious assemblies on the Sabbath, not because they were infected with Judaism, but to worship [Yeshua], the [Master] of the Sabbath, Epiphanius says the same."[8]

Other historians have noted:

"The primitive Christians had a great veneration for the Sabbath and spent the day in devotion and sermons. And it is not to be doubted but they derived this practice from the Apostles themselves, as appears by several scriptures to that purpose."[9]

Another writer contends that the practice of Shabbat is an aid in unity.

"The Sabbath was a strong tie which united them with the life of the whole people, and in keeping the Sabbath holy they followed not only the example but also the command of Jesus."[10]

Gieseler's Church history records that in the second century:

"The Gentile Christians observed also the Sabbath"[11]

An Egyptian papyrus dated to between 200 and 250 CE confirms that Shabbat was still the practice. It reads:

"Except ye make the Sabbath a real Sabbath [sabbatize the Sabbath, Greek], ye shall not see the father." [12]

It is clear from this brief historical record that Shabbat as a matter of faith practice was continued for hundreds of years after the resurrection of the L-rd.

Since the day of rest, Shabbat, was changed from Saturday to Sunday and Sunday is referred to in history as the first day of the week then we can safely assume that Saturday was the seventh day of the week since ancient times.

We can conclude that from Genesis through Revelation and into the 4th century C.E. Shabbat was practiced on the seventh day.

End-time Shabbat

Yeshua was aware that He would be leaving the earth and gave some counsel about the distant future of worship.

Mathew 24: 19-21

Woe to those who are pregnant and to those who are nursing babies in those days! Pray that your escape will not happen in winter, or on Shabbat. For then there will be great trouble, such as has not happened since the beginning of the world until now, nor ever will.

Yeshua spoke of time in the distant future. At the earliest He could have been referring to the destruction of the temple in 70 C.E. But most scholars believe He was referring to the final Armageddon battles that will come. Regardless, He expected Shabbat to be practiced even at that late time.

(Note: there are those who argue that this chapter of the Bible speaks of two different eras. Some argue that this part of the passage refers to those living in Jerusalem rather than the world, but then later in the chapter He speaks more broadly. The passage only makes sense if it is understood from an end- time perspective and thus the persecutions, the false prophets, the good news being proclaimed to the whole world are all precursors to the day that we hope is not a Shabbat.)

Clearly, Yeshua, the apostles and those even in the end of days will have Shabbat on the seventh day and will continue to have it as a key to their faith practice.

Jeff Friedlander

THE SACRED TIME:
A DEEPER LOOK AT THE SEVENTH DAY

G-d modeled Shabbat by taking His rest on the seventh day of the week. Israel and Judah both honored Shabbat on the seventh day. Yeshua, the disciples and the apostles, such as Paul also honored the seventh day Shabbat.

This brings us to a different question. I was asked during one of my teachings, "How do we know that Friday night to Saturday night is the seventh day?" This is an astute question. The Bible doesn't actually name the days of the week, so therefore how can we know Saturday is the seventh day?

I knew this was a critical question that had to have an answer, or the seventh day rest would continue to be defined by mankind. Time measurement in ancient societies was based around the phases of the moon and movement of the sun.

Psalm 104:19

He made the moon to mark the seasons; the sun knows it's time for setting.

Genesis tells us that G-d made the moon, the sun, and the stars for us to mark time. Gen 1:1-16. In fact, one critical point to note is the Hebrew word used for the marking of the season.

Genesis 1:14

Then God said, "Let lights in the expanse of the sky be for separating the day from the night. They will be for signs and for (moadim) **seasons** *and for days and years.*

This word, *moadim,* is used extensively throughout the scriptures and specifically means "appointed times, assembly, appointment." This word is used to describe the marking of a sacred gathering, a feast day, or a Shabbat. Each of these times we are to come together as an assembly to meet as the L-rd has determined. These are appointed times and the timing is known because He put the sun, the moon, and the stars in the sky. We know the evening and morning is marked by the moon and the sun. These are not referring to the marks of the seasons, such as winter, spring, summer or fall only, but also mark the times that G-d has called for us to set apart as sacred.

Who originated the seven-day week?

Modern historians often say that the Biblical seven-day week derived from the Babylonians after the exile period had ended. The Babylonian calendar was used to synchronize the last week of the month with the new moon. Even though the Babylonians created a seven day and monthly calendar, it is now argued that the Jewish calendar pre-dated this. According to Jeffrey H Tigay,

> *"that others before him have concluded that the Biblical Sabbath is mentioned as a day of rest dated to the 9th century B.C.E. This would date it centuries before the Jews were exiled to Babylon. It is clear that among neighboring nations that were in position to have an influence over Israel – and in fact which did influence it in various matters – there is no precise parallel to the Israelite sabbatical week. This leads to the conclusion that the sabbatical week, which is as unique to Israel as the Sabbath from which it flows, is an independent Israelite creation."[1]*

Tigay noted there are differences between the Biblical Sabbath and the Babylonian system, and suggests that the Israelite tradition of a seven-day week is independent of the Babylonian system.

During Roman times, there was a nine-day week in which the days were counted as twelve hours. This did not last and eventually became a seven-day week. "In Rome, the earliest reference to a seven-day week is supposedly from the time of Augustus (27 B.C. – A.D. 14)." [2]

By the fourth century C.E., the seven-day week became the official law. Constantine, in 321, made the Day of the Sun (Sunday) a legal holiday and it was called the first day of the week.

In addition to these evidences of Saturday being the seventh day we can also note the following:

1. The Jewish people have held that the Shabbat is on Saturday from the time of Abraham, and they still keep it that way today.
2. There are over one hundred languages that use a form of Sabbath to distinguish the name of the day Saturday. The Spanish word for "Saturday," for example, is "Sabado," meaning Sabbath. These many languages were developed over thousands of years and Sabbath has always been incorporated into Saturday.
3. The Webster's dictionary defines Saturday as "the seventh day of the week."

From history, we have seen that people including the Jews, the Babylonians, the Romans, and the Christians all chose to name the days, and all had the same conclusion. Saturday was the seventh day.

One may conclude that Saturday being the seventh day is an agreed upon time by all nations, peoples and is historically validated. However, for the skeptic we should note that the evidence of Saturday being the seventh day may be found in the obvious simplicity of the practice of Yeshua. Beyond all the calendar evidence and the historical research, when Messiah Yeshua walked on this earth in the flesh He celebrated the

Shabbat on Saturday. As stated above the Jewish people have kept Shabbat on Saturday since the days of Abraham. There are no historical records to indicate a time when Shabbat was celebrated on a different day. Even today the pattern of keeping Shabbat is on Saturday among all the different Jewish sects. Therefore, when Yeshua, the Jewish man from Galilee celebrated Shabbat, it can be considered with confidence that the day of the week was Saturday.

Luke 4:16-21

And he came to Nazareth, where he had been brought up. And as was his custom, he went to the synagogue on the Sabbath day, and he stood up to read. And the scroll of the prophet Isaiah was given to him. He unrolled the scroll and found the place where it was written,

"The Spirit of the L-rd is upon me, because he has anointed me to proclaim good news to the poor. He has sent me to proclaim liberty to the captives and recovering of sight to the blind, to set at liberty those who are oppressed, to proclaim the year of the L-rd's favor."

And he rolled up the scroll and gave it back to the attendant and sat down. And the eyes of all in the synagogue were fixed on him. And he began to say to them, "Today this Scripture has been fulfilled in your hearing."

Here we see a key phrase, "as was his custom, he went to the synagogue on the Sabbath day and he stood up to read."

We know from multiple external sources and from Jewish sources that the Sabbath practice at the synagogue was on Saturday.

Josephus writes, "There is not any city of the Grecians, nor any of the Barbarians, nor any nation whatsoever, whither our custom of resting on the seventh day hath not come!"[3]

"Philo declares the seventh day to be a festival, not of this or of that city, but of the universe."[4] Before looking at some other historical notes we should address the scriptures that are used to justify a change in the seventh day.

Each of the above references to Shabbat is an inferred reference to Saturday as we have established that history shows only Saturday as the day when the Jews gathered to celebrate Shabbat.

One of the more famous verses quoted as a justification of a Sunday Sabbath is **Acts 20:6-12** (ESV):

*but we sailed away from Philippi after the days of Unleavened Bread, and in five days we came to them at Troas, where we stayed for seven days. On **the first day of the week**, when we were gathered together to break bread, Paul talked with them, intending to depart on the next day, and he prolonged his speech until midnight. There were many lamps in the upper room where we were gathered. And a young man named Eutychus, sitting at the window, sank into a deep sleep as Paul talked still longer. And being overcome by sleep, he fell down from the third story and was taken up dead. But Paul went down and bent over him, and taking him in his arms, said, "Do not be alarmed, for his life is in him." And when Paul had gone up and had broken bread and eaten, he conversed with them a long while, until daybreak, and so departed. And they took the youth away alive and were not a little comforted.*

In English, verse 7 states they were gathered together on the first day of the week to break bread. Many have contended that this verse shows that the New Testament believers were now meeting on the first day of the week and that this is the "day of the L-rd."

This is a tremendous mistranslation. A closer look at the Greek reveals the mistake.

On the first day of the week

μια των σαββατων: mia ton sabaton. The word *mia* translated as first is actually "one." The Greeks used the word *protos* for "first".

The word *sabaton* is not the word for "day of the week." It is the plural of the word Shabbat. Therefore, the correct translation should have been, "one of the Sabbaths." In fact, the word "day" is not in the Greek manuscripts, which must cause us to wonder why the translators would insert the words "day," "first" and "week" into a sentence that does not contain those words. Many have accepted this mistranslation as a truth because it has been conveyed for so many years. Scholars in Greek agree that the correct translation of "mia ton sabaton," is "one of the Sabbaths."

This passage was mistranslated to promote the narrative that Sunday was the "day of the L-rd." We should consider that this gross mistranslation was done to provide a proof text for the moving of Shabbat. In the next chapter, we examine records from the councils of Nicaea and Laodicea, and realize that a greater design to remove all vestiges of Jewish life from the practice of the Christian faith was at work. This came even at the cost of the truth contained in the written word of G-d.

Some who argue for Sunday to be the Sabbath use **1 Corinthians 16:2-3:**

"On the first day of every week, each of you is to put something aside and store it up, as he may prosper, so that there will be no collecting when I come. And when I arrive, I will send those whom you accredit by letter to carry your gift to Jerusalem."

This verse is a confirmation that Paul followed the Torah. He is asking them to prepare the offering of Shavuot. For the purpose of this book, we will not take time to show all the connecting verses, however you may enjoy studying that on your own. Paul is giving instructions which are in line with the Torah. Each one should put away money each week during the time between

Passover and Shavuot (Pentecost) to be prepared for the Leviticus 23:9-14, offering on the Sunday after Passover.

The late Ronald Dart, a Christian author commenting on this subject, noted the following connection between Passover, Crucifixion, and the Sunday after the date.

> *It is clear enough that, in referring to "Christ the first fruits, Paul is referring directly to that first sheaf offered on the morning after the Sabbath by the priest. His wording leaves no room for doubt. James will refer to this as well, "Of his own will begat he us with the word of truth, that we should be a kind of first fruits of his creatures" (James 1:18). What we see here is Christ as the first of the first fruits in the resurrection, with the remainder of the first fruits to follow at his coming.*
>
> *So, this special Sunday after Passover was important to both Jews and Christians. To Jews, it was the day of the offering of the first fruits, the first day of the seven weeks to the Feast of First fruits. To Christians, it was the morning of Jesus' presentation to the Father and of his first appearances to his disciples after his resurrection from the dead. And it was the first day of the seven weeks to Pentecost.*
>
> *For the first Christians, the symbolism of the Jewish observance was seen to point directly to Christ. The connection was clear and strong from the start. The early church had not adopted a calendar different from that of the Jewish majority in the first century. That calendar was crucial, because it defined the time of observance of the feasts. There is not a word in the New Testament to suggest any change from the Jewish observance—so the comparison between liturgy and events was, to them, even more apparent."[5]*

While I do not subscribe to everything Mr. Dart taught, on this point he has it right. There is a special Biblical celebration in operation and Paul is instructing the believers to prepare an offering for this day.

This would be a far reach to conclude that 1 Corinthians 16:2-3 is saying we are to change the day of Shabbat.

Another passage that many use to advocate changing the day of Shabbat is

Romans 14:5-6

"One person esteems one day as better than another, while another esteems all days alike. Each one should be fully convinced in his own mind. The one who observes the day, observes it in honor of the L-rd. The one who eats, eats in honor of the L-rd, since he gives thanks to G-d, while the one who abstains, abstains in honor of the L-rd and gives thanks to G-d."

In context, this verse is about judging a person for their convictions about food. In dealing with a culture that was steeped in worship of idols through food and sacrifice, Paul taught about the proper placement of judgement. Paul argues that each one should have a conviction from the L-rd and honor G-d in that conviction. He says the one who observes "the day" does so in honor of the L-rd. I wonder what day he is referring too? It is a big assumption, one unfair to the text, to state that Paul is telling us to take a Shabbat anytime.

To understand the arguments Paul makes in the New Testament writings when he is referencing the law of Moses, we must have a bit of background on Paul's theology.

Paul fully believed in Torah and observing the Torah. When arrested for his faith Paul gave a strong defense of his beliefs and practice. Acts 21 and 22 he speaks in Hebrew and tells his testimony of salvation. He continues in chapter 23 defending his faith and his practice as a Pharisee who believes in the resurrection of the dead. In chapter 24, Paul is taken before Felix the governor in the city of Caesarea on the coast of the Mediterranean. Here he says that he is innocent and claims to worship G-d according to the sect of Judaism called "the Way." Then he states, "I worship the G-d of our fathers, believing everything laid down by the Law and written in the Prophets." Acts 24:14. He goes even further to show how much he honors the Law of G-d from Torah.

Acts 24:17

Now after several years I came to bring alms to my nation and to present offerings. While I was doing this, they found me purified in the temple, without any crowd or tumult.

Paul argued in his defense,

Acts 25:8

Neither against the law of the Jews, nor against the temple, nor against Caesar have I committed any offense.

He demonstrates that as a follower of Yeshua, an apostle of "the Way," and the apostle to the Gentiles, he walked in observance of the Torah.

As we read Paul's letters to the congregations, we must remember that these letters were written for us but not to us. Paul believed in the Law of Moses, obeyed the law, and committed no offense against it. How could this man who so follows the Torah of Moses ask others to disobey the Torah of Moses? Surely that would not be his desire.

The letters of Paul were written for us but not to us!

Read again the passage through the eyes of Paul and you will quickly be able to sense the bigger message he was trying to communicate.

One final passage that is often cited as proof text that we may change the Shabbat from Saturday to Sunday is **Galatians 4:8-10**

Formerly, when you did not know G-d, you were enslaved to those that by nature are not G-ds. But now that you have come to know G-d, or rather to be known by G-d, how can you turn back again to the weak and worthless elementary principles of the world, whose slaves you want to be once more? You observe days and months and seasons and years! I am afraid I may have labored over you in vain.

What is Paul challenging? Is he challenging the Galatians to abandon the seventh day Sabbath observance or stop celebrating the feasts of the L-rd? Verse 8 makes clear what he is saying. "When you did not know G-d...," then verse 10, "you observe days and months and season and years!" In other words, the days you are now observing are the ones you observed prior to your knowledge of the G-d of Abraham, Isaac, and Jacob. When the Galatians came to faith they came from paganism. They were serving other gods and holding certain days and seasons for those gods. Paul told them to reject false gods and not turn back. This passage has nothing to do with the keeping of Shabbat.

The Galatians had been a very obedient people to the gods they once served and were trying to appease the law as they saw it. But understand—the law never saves. We do not obey the law to be born again but rather we are born again and then moved by the Spirit of G-d to obey the law.

Ezekiel 36:27

I will put My Ruach within you. Then I will cause you to walk in My laws, so you will keep My rulings and do them.

Law obedience will not bring you into salvation. Only blood can make atonement for your sins and only the perfect blood of Yeshua the son of G-d can do that. Faith in Yeshua's sacrifice and resurrection is the only way to be "saved" from the death penalty that awaits all who are lawless or what the Bible calls sinners.

Once we are born again and are part of the family of G-d, the Spirit of G-d guides us into all truth and obedience of G-d's word. His law is good, and His ways are good. Our obedience to those laws brings us closer to knowing Him and understanding Him. Following His ways, statues and laws gives us great joy and brings Him great pleasure. What a joy it must be for the creator to have children who desire to do His word. What a pleasure for our heavenly father to receive when His created children turn to Him and follow His ways.

Shabbat is one of the Ways of G-d. It is His day given to us for our sake and His pleasure. 1 John 2:6 says *whoever says he abides in him ought to walk in the same way in which he walked.*

Yeshua certainly could have changed the day or spoken against it had he wanted to. We should remember that Yeshua was not bashful in speaking against the rules the Pharisees and Sadducees put on the people. He was not shy when it came to challenging the religious rulers of His day. So had He wanted the Shabbat to have been freed from the bonds of a day, the seventh day, He most certainly could have spoken. He did criticize the rules that had been placed on Shabbat, such as not being allowed to heal or eat from the fields when hungry. However, He never once said to practice Shabbat on any day you wish, nor did He grant freedom to pick a different observance day. Shabbat is the seventh day, Saturday, and it is a sacred day. It is to be holy and set apart. This day is not permitted to be just any day. This is a holy day. This is a sacred day.

The question that I get asked more than any other on this subject and the one that you may have right now. "Didn't Jesus say the Sabbath was made for man and not man made for the sabbath? If so, then can't I determine when I want to have the sabbath since it was made for me? Also, since Jesus was raised on the first day of the week, if I was going to pick a sabbath day shouldn't it be Sunday?"

These are not only thoughtful questions; they are good questions. Let's look at them from a Biblical point of view and then I want to share a piece of my heart with you on this matter.

The book of Mark illuminates Sabbath keeping practices:

Mark 2:23-27

One Sabbath he was going through the grainfields, and as they made their way, his disciples began to pluck heads of grain. And the Pharisees were saying to him, "Look, why are they doing what is not lawful on the Sabbath?" And he said to them, "Have you never read what David did, when he was in need and was hungry, he and those who were with him: how he entered the house of G-d, in the time of Abiathar the high priest, and ate the bread of the Presence, which it is not lawful for any but the priests to eat, and also gave it to those who were with him?" And he said to them, "The Sabbath was made for man, not man for the Sabbath. So the Son of Man is L-rd even of the Sabbath."

This passage has been used to change the power of the law of G-d. Simply put, people have used these words to say that G-d gave us the power to define and determine all aspects surrounding Shabbat including the day. Some say, "If the Shabbat was made for man and not man for the Shabbat and that was the justification to eat the bread of presence or the justification for Yeshua and disciples to gather food in the grainfields, then certainly we may choose to do whatever we wish on Shabbat and we may choose to change the time of Shabbat."

Is this seeking the heart of G-d or the power and independence of man? Yeshua stated, in defense of taking a restricted practice of gathering food on Shabbat or eating the bread of presence as King David did, that Shabbat is a gift from G-d, a blessing, and therefore the Shabbat should be a day when mankind is taken care of. But the closing argument He uses is the key. "Shabbat was made for man and therefore the SON of MAN is L-rd of the Shabbat." Who is this Son of Man? More than that...who is the

L-rd of the Shabbat? It is the Messiah, Yeshua. You and I are not the L-rd of the day! Yeshua is. He had a right to change the day of keeping the Shabbat had he wanted to. He did not. He is L-rd.

Adam Clarke comments on this verse:

> "That he might have the seventh part of his whole time to devote to the purposes of bodily rest and spiritual exercises. And in these respects it is of infinite use to mankind. Where no Sabbath is observed, there disease, poverty, and profligacy, generally prevail. Had we no Sabbath, we should soon have no religion."[6]

Shabbat was made for man. Meaning simply Shabbat was meant to always be a blessing to man rather than a burden. During this first century, the leaders in Israel had added many layers of law and regulation around the Shabbat to make sure that it was protected. They had missed the true value of Shabbat in their zeal to protect the people and the law. The fact is that neither Yeshua nor his disciples had stepped outside of any Torah command to observe the Shabbat. The Bible does not anywhere state that one cannot pick food when needed to eat or walk on Shabbat. Nor does the Bible say that man has the right to change the day and time of Shabbat. G-d appointed the time and I pray that all of us may become obedient to His time.

Jeff Friedlander

WHO MOVED SHABBAT?

Although scripture is clear we must also contend with history. Many have been told that after the resurrection the church began to worship on Sunday to honor it as the day of the L-rd. However, this was not true in the early years after resurrection. As we have shown, Paul certainly went to synagogue on Shabbat regularly and that is where his ministry took place. This was on the seventh day. He never encouraged the congregations he formed to change the day of worship from Saturday to Sunday.

This change from seventh day observance starting on Friday evening and ending on Saturday evening was intentional and anti-Semitic. Men made the decision to change the day G-d created in Genesis and called the Shabbat to a different day. Men became their own god. That is a painful realization. There is not a single scriptural or early record of the first followers of Messiah to the last living apostle, John, changing the day of Shabbat from Saturday to Sunday.

We are going to look at the historical record and see the councils of the church that changed the practice of Shabbat. The councils made a law that no one may practice Shabbat on Saturday.

If Shabbat was already in widespread practice on Sunday rather than Saturday, then there would have been no need to make such a law.

How did we come to practice Shabbat on Sunday? Or for that matter, why do some even take another day and call it Shabbat?

Sunday has been the accepted day of gathering for Christians since the fourth century. Growing up I was never introduced to another way to come together with other believers than on Sunday.

There are many who observe and deeply cherish the belief that the Shabbat is actually on Sunday because Messiah arose from the dead-on Sunday, therefore He must have established Shabbat to be on Sunday. As we will discover, the Bible is true, but our traditions are not always right.

I was once asked by a dear Baptist brother if meeting together for church on Sunday was wrong or a sin. I told him of course it was not wrong or a sin. Yeshua even told us that where two or three are gathered together G-d is in their midst. We can certainly meet and worship any day of the week. Meeting together is not the problem. The way we inherited the Sunday meeting and the theology we hold to is the problem.

If Shabbat is clearly the seventh day and Yeshua, the Apostles and the early believing communities continued to practice Shabbat on Saturday, up to 300 years after the resurrection, then WHY and when did it change to Sunday?

The answer is one word: ROME! Recorded history illuminates the loss of the Shabbat light:

I want to underscore the reason for the change. Rome made a change in the practice of Shabbat (and other Jewish customs) for the simple fact that they hated the Jews and wanted to distance the Christian faith from Judaism at all cost. This is painful to hear but it is true. The history is clear.

The 17th century historian William Cave writes that the early Christians and Jews were keeping Shabbat on Saturdays:

> "For this reason, it seemed good to the prudence of those times, (as in others of the Jewish rites, so in this,) to indulge the humor of that people, and to keep the sabbath as a day for religious offices. Hence, they usually had most parts of the divine service performed upon that day;

they met together for public prayers, for reading the scriptures, celebration of the sacraments, and such like duties. This is plain, not only from some passages in Ignatius and Clemens's Constitutions, but from writers of more unquestionable credit and authority. Athanasius, bishop of Alexandria, tells us, that they assembled on *Saturdays*, not that they were infected with Judaism, but only to worship Jesus Christ, the L-rd of the sabbath."[1] (emphasis mine)

The author, who wrote this in the mid 1800's, uses the anti-Semitic phrase "infected with Judaism." It was and still is very common to look through the lens of history and see hatred and bigotry toward the Jewish people. This historian notes for us that the early Christians were celebrating Saturday as Shabbat, but wanted to make sure it was known to the reader that these same Christians had not been "infected" by the Jewish religion or people. This is a key to understanding the changing of the Shabbat from a sacred practice on Saturday to a Sunday morning worship service.

The first known reference to a non-Saturday Shabbat was by Marcion in Rome. Marcion was the bishop of an area in what is now northwest Turkey. He was born around 110 CE. Around 144 CE, he founded a group that was heretical in its teachings and practice, and which was in 155 CE denounced by Polycarp of Smyrna.

"Marcion acquired his very perverse opinions not from a master, but his master from his opinion! He displayed a hatred against the Jews' most solemn day, He was only professedly following the Creator, as being His Christ, in this very hatred of the Sabbath..."[2]

"Marcion who fasted on the Sabbath to show his contempt for the G-d of the Old Testament whom he considered to be evil."[3]

Another source tells us:

> "Expounding on Paul's characterization of the Mosaic Law as the cause of sin, Marcion desired a Christianity untainted by any elements of Judaism. He saw the G-d of the Old Testament as cruel and vengeful, an embarrassment and a stumbling block in the evangelization of the Gentiles. He charged that the Church had erred in clinging to the Old Testament, that the gospel had completely superseded the Torah, and that the apostles, except Paul, had allowed their Jewish notions to corrupt the message of the loving G-d. He rejected all the books of the Old Testament and retained only those of the New which were clearly authored by Paul, purging any texts which conflicted with his personal beliefs. He mandated fasting on Saturday in opposition to the G-d of the Jewish Sabbath." [4]

This was one of the early leaders of the Christian world. Thank G-d others denounced him as a heretic. However, some of his ideas were planted as seeds and eventually those seeds grew. (We even hear some of his words today through modern preachers. A pastor of a mega church recently claimed that we must "unhitch" ourselves from the Old Testament completely just as the disciples did. Very Marcionite.)

> "Justin Martyr, (100-165) who attended worship on the first day, wrote about the cessation of Hebrew Sabbath observance and stated that the Sabbath was enjoined as a temporary sign to Israel to teach of human sinfulness (Gal. 3:24-25), no longer needed after Christ came without sin. He rejected the need to keep literal seventh-day Sabbath, arguing instead that "the new law requires you to keep the sabbath constantly." With Christian corporate worship so clearly aligned with the Eucharist and allowed on the seventh day, Hebrew Sabbath

practices primarily involved the observance of a day of rest. He rejected the need to keep literal seventh-day Sabbath, arguing instead that "the new law requires you to keep the sabbath constantly."[5]

Ignatius (35-108) wrote "Let us therefore no longer keep the Sabbath after the Jewish manner, and rejoice in days of idleness. But let every one of you keep the Sabbath after a spiritual manner, rejoicing in meditation on the law, not in relaxation of the body, admiring the workmanship of G-d, and not eating things prepared the day before, nor using lukewarm drinks, and walking within a prescribed space, nor finding delight in dancing and plaudits which have no sense in them. And after the observance of the Sabbath, let every friend of Christ keep the L-rd's [Day, *Dominicam*] as a festival, the resurrection-day, the queen and chief of all the days." [6]

Clearly, the seeds of the heretic Marcion had grown regarding a seventh Day Shabbat. However, even while the Gentile growth of the church was happening, and the catholic church was solidifying its systems, there were those who still admitted to the practice of a seventh day as the way.

The Eastern Orthodox today practice Sunday worship yet do admit the following: "At first, early Jewish Christians continued to observe Sabbath regulations and to worship on the Sabbath… (Acts 13:13-15, 42-44; 18:1-4) …for Orthodox Christians, **Saturday is still the Sabbath**, the day on which the Church especially remembers the departed since Christ rested in the tomb on Great and Holy Saturday."[7]

Here are a few other historical references to the early practice.

SPAIN – Council Elvira (A.D. 305)

Canon 26 of the Council of Elvira reveals that the Church of Spain at that time kept Saturday, the seventh day. "As to fasting every Sabbath: Resolved, that the error be corrected of fasting every Sabbath." This resolution of the council is in direct opposition to the policy the church at Rome had inaugurated, that of commanding Sabbath as a fast day in order to humiliate it and make it repugnant to the people.

PERSIA – A.D. 335-375

"They despise our sun G-d. Did not Zoroaster, the sainted founder of our divine beliefs, institute Sunday one thousand years ago in honour of the sun and supplant the Sabbath of the Old Testament. Yet these Christians have divine services on Saturday."[8]

Shabbat was a Saturday celebration around the world except in Rome. In fact, the saying "When in Rome…" originates from the change of the Shabbat from Saturday to Sunday. "Ambrose, the celebrated bishop of Milan, said that when he was in Milan he observed Saturday, but when in Rome observed Sunday. This gave rise to the proverb 'When you are in Rome, do as Rome does,'" [9]

However, the Bishop Ambrose, was an anti-Semite as were many church leaders of the fourth century:

> "Ambrose was far from a fan of the Jewish people or the way of the Jewish religion. He writes the emperor who has commanded that a synagogue which was burned by Christians be repaired by Ambrose and the church. To defend the actions and deny the request Ambrose in part writes "There is, then, no adequate cause for such a commotion, that the people should be so severely punished for the burning of a building, and much less since it is the burning of a synagogue, a home of unbelief, a house of impiety, a receptacle of folly, which G-d Himself has condemned. For thus we read, where the L-rd our G-d speaks by the mouth of the prophet Jeremiah: "And I will do to this house, which is called by My Name,

wherein ye trust, and to the place which I gave to you and to your fathers, as I have done to Shiloh, and I will cast you forth from My sight, as I cast forth your brethren, the whole seed of Ephraim. And do not thou pray for that people, and do not thou ask mercy for them, and do not come near Me on their behalf, for I will not..."[10]

The leaders of the Roman church were disinclined to accept any practice of the Jews. They hated the people and anything that related to them. They justified this hatred by using scriptures to prove the Jews had disobeyed G-d and deserved the punishment the Roman church would bring. They believed they were the instruments that G-d wanted to use to purify the Jews.

They wanted to do something different and make a distinction between the Christian religion and the Jewish religion. Moving worship from Saturday to Sunday and calling it the Sabbath seemed logical. And historically, the Romans had for years worshiped deities on Sunday.

J.N. Andrews in "History of the Sabbath" states:

"The festival of Sunday is more ancient than the Christian religion, its origin being lost in remote antiquity. It did not originate, however, from any divine command nor from piety toward G-d: on the contrary, it was set apart as a sacred day by the heathen world in honor of their chief G-d, the sun. It is from this fact that the first day of the week has obtained the name of Sunday, a name by which it is known in many languages."[11]

Sunday was a day for pagan worship of the sun, as noted by Andrews:

"In the time of Justin Martyr, Sunday was a weekly festival, widely celebrated by the heathen in honor of their G-d, the sun. And so, in presenting to the heathen emperor of Rome an "Apology" for his brethren, Justin takes care to tell him thrice that the Christians held their assemblies on this day of general observance. Sunday therefore makes its first appearance in the Christian church as an institution identical in time with the weekly festival of the heathen, and Justin, who first mentions this festival, had been a heathen philosopher. Sixty years later, Tertullian acknowledges that it was not without an appearance of truth that men declared the sun to be the G-d of the Christians. But he answered that though they worshiped toward the east like the heathen, and devoted Sunday to rejoicing, it was for a reason far different from sun-worship."

History records that early believers kept the Sabbath on the seventh day but with increasing persecution from the Romans, they began to acquiesce to the Roman day of rest mandated by man to be Sunday. Their acquiescence staved off the coming persecution.

"When Emperor Constantine I—a pagan sun-worshipper—came to power in A.D. 313, he legalized Christianity and made the first Sunday-keeping law. His infamous Sunday enforcement law of March 7, A.D. 321, reads as follows: "On the venerable Day of the Sun let the magistrates and people residing in cities rest, and let all workshops be closed."" [12]

It is noted that with this decree the name was also changed from the "Venerable day of the sun" to "The L-rd's day."

The Council of Nicaea determined that the day of resurrection was more important than the day the L-rd commanded to be called the Shabbat.

In 325 C.E. the Council of Nicaea proclaimed dramatic anti-Semitic changes. Three hundred and eighteen bishops attended the council. It is unfortunate, and no doubt intentional, that no Jewish leaders were invited. The conclusions of the council were that all the churches should celebrate Easter on the Sunday following the first full moon which occurs after the spring equinox. The laws of the scriptures had already been overturned by this time and now they were taking it a step further.

In his letter to the churches Constantine makes sure all understand the bishops' unanimous sentiments:

> At the council we also considered the issue of our holiest day, Easter, and it was determined by common consent that everyone, everywhere should celebrate it on one and the same day. For what can be more appropriate, or what more solemn, than that this feast from which we have received the hope of immortality, should be kept by all without variation, using the same order and a clear arrangement? And in the first place, it seemed very unworthy for us to keep this most sacred feast following the custom of the Jews, a people who have soiled their hands in a most terrible outrage, and have thus polluted their souls, and are now deservedly blind. Since we have cast aside their way of calculating the date of the festival, we can ensure that future generations can celebrate this observance at the more accurate time which we have kept from the first day of the passion until the present time. Therefore, have nothing in common with that most hostile people, the Jews. We have received another way from the Savior. In our holy religion we have set before us a course which is both valid and accurate. Let us unanimously pursue this. Let us, most honored brothers, withdraw ourselves from that detestable association. It is truly most absurd for them to boast that we are incapable of rightly observing these things without their instruction. On what subject are they competent to form a correct judgment, who, after that murder of their L-rd lost their senses, and are led not by any rational motive, but by an uncontrollable impulsiveness to wherever their innate fury may drive them? This is why even in this matter they

do not perceive the truth, so that they constantly err in the utmost degree, and will celebrate the Feast of Passover a second time in the same year instead of making a suitable correction. Why then should we follow the example of those who are acknowledged to be infected with serious error? Surely, we should never allow Easter to be kept twice in one and the same year! But even if these considerations were not laid before you, you should still be careful, both by diligence and prayer, that your pure souls should have nothing in common, or even seem to do so, with the customs of men so utterly depraved.[14]

The day was changed for political, anti-Semitic, and controlling reasons.

We also know this is true because of the Roman law that would come out in 364 C.E. A council of the Eastern church met in Laodicea and declared in Canon 29:

"Christians must not Judaize by resting on the Sabbath, but must work on that day, rather honoring the L-rd's Day; and, if they can, resting then as Christians. But if any shall be found to be Judaizes, let them be anathema from Christ."[13]

When the council outlawed rest on Saturday they were coming directly against those that were practicing the Saturday Shabbat. This must have been a widespread practice to necessitate a canon forbidding it! Also, this was a culmination of a strong and centuries long antisemitic heart. The church had long been letting the seeds of the excommunicated heretic Maricon grow and now they were in full bloom.

We should be aware that the councils of Nicaea and Laodicea had no Jewish representation. The laws decreed from these councils were anti-Semitic and were not only designed to change the Biblical command but were a result of the blame the Catholic church had laid upon the Jewish people for the killing of Christ.

The genesis of the practice of Shabbat on Sunday has been obscured. After thousands of years of celebrating on Sunday, many assume it is an acceptable Biblical practice and therefore have never questioned it. For most people this is difficult to hear. Sunday worship has been such a tradition and is so entrenched into the fabric of the church that the idea of it being built on a foundation other than scripture is difficult. However, in order for us to walk in truth we must be willing to face the truth.

Although we could go on and on with historical writings about the practice of Shabbat being on Saturday, the seventh day of the week and about the transition away from that day, this book is not an academic historical thesis. Rather, I wanted to give you enough information to stir your thoughts and your hearts that you may return to the Bible as the only real source of our teaching. We must hold to the Bible and what it tells us to do regarding Shabbat.

The protestant movement uses a phrase "Solo Scriptura" which is Latin for "Only Scripture." The idea being conveyed is that the Protestants, unlike the Catholics whom they broke away from, will only listen to the scripture. Scripture is to be the ruling guide rather than the Pope, bishops, or cardinals. In addition, Protestants will not listen to the Pharisees, the Jewish Sages nor the Talmud. In other words, the Protestants have moved the faith back on "good ground" with the idea of solo scriptura…or so they say.

When one looks at the subject of Shabbat, we find a critical divide between the principle of solo scriptura and actual practice.

Note the following from Catholic Priest Reverend John A. O'Brien:

> "… the Bible does not contain all the teachings of the Christian religion, nor does it: formulate all the duties of its members. Take, for example, the matter of Sunday observance, the attendance at divine services and the

abstention from unnecessary servile work on that day, a matter upon which our Protestant neighbors have for many years laid great emphasis. Let me address myself in a friendly spirit to my dear Protestant reader: You believe that the Bible alone is a safe guide in religious matters. You also believe that one of the fundamental duties enjoined upon you by your Christian faith is that of Sunday observance. But where does the Bible speak of such an obligation? I have read the Bible from the first verse of Genesis to the last verse of Revelations and have found no reference to the duty of sanctifying the Sunday. The day mentioned in the Bible is not the Sunday, the first day of the week, but the Saturday, the last day of the week. It was the Apostolic Church which, acting by virtue of that authority conferred upon her by Christ, changed the observance to the Sunday in honor of the day on which Christ rose from the dead, and to signify that now we are no longer under the Old Law of the Jews, but under the New Law of Christ. In observing the Sunday as you do, is it not apparent that you are really acknowledging the insufficiency of the Bible alone as a rule of faith and religious conduct, and proclaiming the need of a divinely established teaching authority which in theory you deny?"[15]

O'Brien highlights distinctions between Catholicism and Protestantism, using the Bible as confirmation. First, Reverend O'Brien confirms that the Bible never teaches one to observe the first day of the week as Shabbat. It was always the seventh day of the week according to the Bible. Second, he distinguishes that it was the Catholic Church who determined to change the day to Sunday and did so because they believed that the authority to change the scripture lies within the Roman Catholic Church. He stated clearly that the Bible does not change the command to practice the seventh day as Shabbat but then states plainly that the church was given power to change G-d's commands. This seems to be a distinct difference between the Catholic belief and the Protestant belief. Yet he points out that the Protestants may not be as different as one thinks. For them to practice a first day of the week Shabbat rather than a seventh day of the week shows that the Protestants are under the rules of Rome rather than the rules of the Bible. They have been following the Catholic popes' decisions to change the scripture and they do not even know it.

Our review of history confirms that Saturday is the seventh day, and it is holy, sacred and appointed by G-d Himself. Let's briefly revisit the key scriptures.

Leviticus 23:1-3

The L-rd spoke to Moses, saying, "Speak to the people of Israel and say to them: These are the appointed feasts of the L-rd that you shall proclaim as holy convocations; they are my appointed feasts.

Six days shall work be done, but on the seventh day is a Sabbath of solemn rest, a holy convocation. You shall do no work. It is a Sabbath to the L-rd in all your dwelling places.

These are the "appointed feast" of the L-rd. The first one listed is the weekly Shabbat. This is an appointment that G-d has set with His people. We are His people, not because we are Jewish by ethnicity or Jewish by claim of faith but rather, we are His people because we are followers of Yeshua the Messiah of G-d. We have faith in the blood for forgiveness of our sins and rebirth. This makes us the promised seed of Abraham and children of G-d. We are the ones to whom these appointed feasts are written, too.

This part of the Bible was not written for just a desert dwelling people of the ancient past. This part was written for those who do what Jesus did. We keep Shabbat on the Seventh Day because it is an appointed time that is called holy by G-d himself.

Genesis 2:1-3

Thus, the heavens and the earth were finished, and all the host of them. And on the seventh day G-d finished his work that he had done, and he rested on the seventh day from all his work that he had done. So G-d blessed the seventh day and made it holy, because on its G-d rested from all his work that he had done in creation.

Exodus 20:8-11

*Remember the Sabbath day, to keep it holy. Six days you shall labor, and do all your work, but the seventh day is a Sabbath to the L-rd your G-d. On it you shall not do any work, you, or your son, or your daughter, your male servant, or your female servant, or your livestock, or the sojourner who is within your gates. **For in six days the L-rd made heaven and earth, the sea, and all that is in them, and rested on the seventh day. Therefore, the L-rd blessed the Sabbath day and made it holy.***

Why does G-d care about the day? He made all of creation in the previous six days and on this seventh day He looked over and admired His work. He called it good. This day is the day He blessed and made holy. So, we are to do the same thing every seven days. On the seventh day we look over G-d's creation and are reminded of His goodness and His power. We are reminded of our creator and humbled that we are chosen to be a part of His creation. We spend the sacred time in awe of this all-powerful G-d who has brought us into His light. This sacred day is holy and if we should choose to guard and keep it as commanded then G-d has promised to bless us. He has promised to be there with us for His appointed time.

Yes, we most certainly can worship G-d on any day of the week. In fact, I would suggest that we should worship G-d every day of the week, for all our waking hours and then we should ask for dreams from Him. We are not limited to one day of worship and dedication. Quite the opposite. This Shabbat gives us time to reflect and refresh so that we may spend the other six days being the light and reflecting His glory to the earth.

Relationships are built by regular and consistent communication. Our relationship with G-d is no different. But just as my wife and I have a date night each week to specifically focus on our marriage, I still talk to her the other six nights of the week. I do not celebrate my anniversary with her one day a year and ignore our marriage the other 364 days. In the same way, each week on the seventh day we take sacred time and focus on the creation and the Creator, and our family and friends. The other six days we grow and move the spiritual needle forward.

In summary, the Saturday seventh day is holy and each of us will benefit from serving a benevolent King in the way He has commanded. We, to our own detriment, choose to serve our G-d on our terms. Make the change today. Begin to guard and keep the seventh day Shabbat this week. When you honor G-d's Shabbat on the Sacred Day He chose, He will honor you.

Intro to the Sacred Rest!

Shabbat is sacred. Gathering together on Sunday to go to church is certainly not forbidden by G-d but making it Shabbat is. Church history, as with any history, is a mixed bag. While the Christian church has been a catalyst for benevolence and charity it has also been a force for death and violence. The church, like any organization made up of people, has flaws and glories. Reading church history can sometimes become a bitter pill to swallow.

Theology is the study of G-d in the text-book definition. Beyond that, for most people theology is the way they come to understand G-d and man's relationship to Him. From that viewpoint, we realize that people frame a theology fairly early in life. This becomes difficult to shift and adjust as one ages.

My wife was raised in a southern Baptist tradition. Her church leaned heavily on Bible reading and evangelism. They preached the gospel of salvation through Jesus. However, in her tradition, Jesus never appeared Jewish. In fact, the writings of the Bible were read and interpreted from a western and yes, even southern worldview. This worldview did not allow for the Jewishness of Yeshua to come forth or even be known. Although this may have not been intentional it came with consequence. When Sherri discovered the Jewishness of the Messiah, she had to do some significant soul searching and reckoning. Although the doctrine of salvation and the basic truth of main doctrines had not changed, many other things did. Those things brought a challenge to her worldview and her way of understanding the Bible.

When new information is revealed about the Bible, G-d, or faith practice, internal struggle will almost inevitably result. When your tradition or mindset faces new information, battle lines often get drawn. My encouragement is simple: pray and invite the Holy Spirit of G-d to be your teacher. **John 14:26** reminds us that,

"But the Helper, the Ruach ha-Kodesh whom the Father will send in My name, will teach you everything and remind you of everything that I said to you."

It is important not to stand against His word for the sake of a tradition. Stand only for His truth as it is given by the Spirit through the word. This must be the plumb line. Allow the truth of history and the truth of G-d's word to reframe your mindset and become a part of the unfolding story of Restoring the Sacred.

SHABBAT AND THE SACREDNESS OF FAMILY

The heart of the Father is family. In Genesis, right after establishing the Shabbat, G-d spoke into creation the simple yet profound way He expects humans on the earth to function and thrive, through family.

Genesis 2:1-3

Thus, the heavens and the earth were finished, and all the host of them. And on the seventh day G-d finished his work that he had done, and he rested on the seventh day from all his work that he had done. So, G-d blessed the seventh day and made it holy, because on it G-d rested from all his work that he had done in creation.

G-d rested. We then read the second telling of the creation of Man and Woman. Genesis chapter 2 retells the creation story with some additional bits of information. **Genesis 2:18** reveals G-d's intentions for Adam.

Then the L-rd G-d said, "It is not good that the man should be alone; I will make him a helper fit for him."

At this point in the narrative, Adam has seen the living creatures that G-d created and is looking for a helper suitable to be with him. G-d addresses that Adam needs companionship. What was the remedy?

Genesis 2:21

So the L-rd G-d caused a deep sleep to fall upon the man, and while he slept took one of his ribs and closed up its place with flesh. And the rib that the L-rd G-d had taken from the man he made into a woman and brought her to the man. Then the man said,

"This at last is bone of my bones and flesh of my flesh; she shall be called Woman, because she was taken out of Man."

Therefore a man shall leave his father and his mother and hold fast to his wife, and they shall become one flesh. And the man and his wife were both naked and were not ashamed.

G-d creates a woman for the man and together they will form a partnership of marriage. This marriage, a husband (man) and a wife (woman) establish the boundaries for the greatest intimacy a person can have on the earth with another person. This creation of family was the solution to isolation.

Let me note that if you are single, you are not incomplete nor exempt from a partnership. While you wait for your spouse, or remain single by choice, you can find fulfillment in community. Isolation is a forced sense of being alone; but G-d does not isolate you.

This planet the L-rd created is His, as are all that dwell here. Even those who reject Him. *Psalm 24:1[1]*

On His planet, He desires each of us to be connected to each other and the primary connection begins in the nuclear family with husband and wife. Although our society today is fragmented through divorce, babies being born outside of marriage covenants, and the redefinition of Biblical marriage, we have hope in the message of redemption.

Be encouraged. We are part of the amazing story of redemption. We read in the garden narrative that even the original first family blew it. First, they disobeyed G-d and ate from the tree of the knowledge of good and evil. Second, they had children who were disobedient and caused them great pain to the extent that one child murdered the other one. So be encouraged that G-d has a plan for each of our dysfunctions and can move through them to redeem our family, regardless of its current condition.

That said, let me elevate the discussion. G-d's incontrovertible plan for family plan was laid out in creation.

When G-d said he was going to create man in Genesis 1:26-27, He used the word אָדָם *adam*. This word means mankind or human being. It is a term used to describe all of us.

*Then G-d said, "Let Us make **man (Adam)** in Our image, after Our likeness! Let them rule over the fish of the sea, over the flying creatures of the sky, over the livestock, over the whole earth, and over every crawling creature that crawls on the land."*

*G-d created humankind in His image, in the image of G-d He created him, **male (zakar)** and **female** (něqebah) He created them.*

Notice in Verse 27, when he creates a male, he uses the word זָכָר *zakar* rather than Adam and the word נְקֵבָה *něqebah* for female. He makes a clear distinction between male and female.

The text takes us back to the idea of mankind from which G-d next creates אִשָּׁה *ishah* which is the woman.

Mankind is adam and can be thought of to be male or female depending on the context of the passage of scripture. אִישׁ *Ish* is male and אִשָּׁה *Ishah* is female and carry the distinctiveness of biology and sexuality.

Genesis 2:24-25 gives us the full picture of G-d's first human family:

Therefore a man (אִישׁ ish) shall leave his father and his mother and hold fast to his wife (אִשָּׁה ishah), and they shall become one flesh. And the man (אָדָם adam) and his wife (אִשָּׁה ishah) were both naked and were not ashamed.

Here we see all the words and the distinctions. Man, in the context of marriage is male and woman in the context of marriage is female. This is G-d's family plan.

Is it any wonder that the G-d ordained union is the major assault of the enemy? The Satan's strategy is to destroy that which G-d created and called very good. This is an age-old tactic, in fact, history records that at the core of all fallen empires is the fall of the family. When the family, husband, wife, and children, fall into decline through divorce, redefinition, and moral confusion, the empire will fall.

G-d's earth was designed to be managed by the family of G-d. His family belongs to him first and to each other second. But we partner with G-d to establish His kingdom on earth and bring Him back as King. Today, we are watching a rapid decline in family. The stats are overwhelming.

Single family homes due to divorce and children being born outside of wed- lock are at all-time highs and increasing. The CDC reports that there are 39.9 births per 1,000 unmarried women aged 15-44 as of March 2021.[2]

This means 4 out of 10 children or almost half of the children born in America today have only a single mom to raise them.

Divorce was once thought of as unacceptable by most of the body of believers. Many couples would fight to keep from a divorce because of the damage to children and the shame associated with it. Today it is reduced from Holy to a punchline for a comedian. It is more commonly assumed that someone has been married and divorced than not. A question that singles or recently divorced find themselves asking is, "So, how many times have you been married?"

Divorce has become a normal part of the personal narratives. These narratives don't often reveal the pain that accompanies a divorce. Deviating from G-d's plan leaves us with an emptiness and dissatisfaction that is intangible. The church has done a disservice to marriage by seemingly giving a stamp of approval to divorce. Our marriage small groups should be fuller in attendance than our divorce recovery groups.

To the millions of you that have been through divorce, I say loud and clear BE NOT ASHAMED OR CONDEMMED! Your situation may have merited divorce. For example, when adultery is involved or when violence is involved G-d would certainly grant the certificate of divorce as stated in Matthew 5:32.[3]

Regardless of why you are divorced you must never walk-in shame if you are a follower of Yeshua the Messiah. He came that you may be set free from shame. He is the REDEEMER! He takes that which has been painful or even sinful and turns it into righteousness. He removes the stain of the divorce that you may be made new in His image. Let not yourself walk in condemnation of any type. G-d LOVES you and G-d will empower you to live the life He destined for you. "For all have sinned and fallen short of the glory of G-d." Romans 3:23. Even if your divorce was not for the "right" reason, G-d still wants to partner with you as a member of His family.

That all being said, we must endeavor to fight for the what the Bible teaches. We do not have the authority to change the Bible. It is what it is!

G-d wants family and that begins with a male and female. The devil wants chaos and pain that begins with divorce, sexual immorality and now redefining the word marriage. This chaos ushers in a very dysfunctional and society that crushes the citizens within.

When G-d made family, he gave us a picture of how we are to steward the planet he created. Therefore, it would make sense for Him to give us a way to take care of family so that we would be healthy and able to manage His planet. The kingdom of G-d functions best through healthy families.

In the book of Exodus, we read an amazing phrase that many would have thought was New Testament.

Exodus 19:6

*...and you shall be to me a **kingdom of priests** and a holy nation.' These are the words that you shall speak to the people of Israel.*

He is speaking to the people of Israel and identifying their role in the kingdom as priests and a holy nation. He speaks to them as a company comprised of families and individuals. He states that they are to be a "kingdom of priests." What a phrase. Imagine you and I are part of the Kingdom that G-d created, and we are His priests in this kingdom. We are the people that represent and grow His kingdom in His planet.

This kingdom of priests is echoed again in the New Testament.

1 Peter 2:9 (ESV)

*But you are a chosen race, **a royal priesthood**, a holy nation, a people for his own possession, that you may proclaim the excellencies of him who called you out of darkness into his marvelous light.*

Here Peter calls out all believers as a royal priesthood, a chosen nation. G-d is taking a people, composed of individuals, and making them a nation.

Revelation 1:6 (ESV)

And made us a kingdom, priests to his G-d and Father, to him be glory and dominion forever and ever. Amen.

Here we see that G-d makes us a kingdom, which is an indicator of our role as priest. Again and again, we see confirmation of our priesthood in scripture.

A Family that Rests Together...The Power of Shabbat in a family!

The affirmation of family is a purposeful intent of G-d's weekly calendar. G-d created man and woman on the sixth day and then followed that day with a day of rest. Each week G-d knew we would need a time to gather with our family and worship together and refresh our souls with Him. Our home would be the holy of holies and the Shabbat would be a weekly time of entering into that most sacred place of the presence of G-d as a family. What would our communities be like if most families were keeping Shabbat each seventh day and connecting around the table of our King?

One of the greatest outcomes of restoring Sabbath to its proper place and practice is the restoration of family. Imagine each week bringing your family together for an intentional meal and time of blessing. Let your own imagination flow for a moment. Dream a little with G-d and begin to sense the amazing things that could happen around the table. Good things happen around the table.

During a weekly home Shabbat there are customs that can be useful in providing unity in the family and the community. These customs connect us to each other and, in a sense, to the extended world around us. For example, when we light the Shabbat candles on Friday evening to signify the beginning of Shabbat, we are in unity with the millions around the globe who are doing the same thing. More than that we are in unity with the families of the past as some of these customs have been practiced for thousands of years. Each of these can be a beautiful connection point to G-d and each other.

One of the customs of Shabbat is for the head of the house to bless the family. (The head of the house is the husband. Where a husband is not present the mother takes the role. A single person is obviously the head of that home. Singles can and should look for others to gather with and build a community together. Go to www.beonetoday.org for more information.)

What are some of the blessings that can be used?

These have been gathered and edited from many different groups that practice Shabbat. There is no requirement Biblically to do these or to use the ones we list. They are simply a tool to help in your Shabbat celebration. Although not required, imagine millions of people each Friday evening speaking these blessings over their families. What a difference this could make.

BLESSING OVER THE HOME

Avinu Malkeinu (Our Father and King)

Just as Solomon dedicated the temple to You, I dedicate this home and property to You. (1 Kings 8). It shall be a house of prayer, a house of praise and worship to You my L-rd. May all that is done within the walls and property of this house be used to glorify You L-rd. Like Joshua before me, I declare that "As for me and my house, we will serve the L-rd. Joshua 24:15. B'shem Yeshua (In the name of Jesus)

PRAYER FOR MARRIAGE

Avinu Malkeinu (Our Father and King)

Just as you brought Adam and Eve together and blessed their union, Father we ask Your blessing on our marriage. We invite You to be the center of this marriage. We acknowledge that apart from You we can do nothing (John 15:5). We ask You L-rd, to show us how to be considerate of one another's needs and wishes and feelings (Ephesians 5:21-33). Help us to be understanding and forgiving of one another's weaknesses. Help us to walk in forgiveness always remembering that You have forgiven us (Ephesians 4:32) Help us to show Your mercy and grace to each other and to keep no record of past hurts or failures (1 Corinthians 13:5). Thank you, Father, for my spouse. We believe You have called us together to glorify You and serve You. B'shem Yeshua (In the name of Jesus)

PRAYER FOR CHILDREN

Avinu Malkeinu (Our Father and King)

Make your face shine upon my children and be gracious unto them. Lift up Your countenance upon them and give them peace. (Numbers 6:23-26) I pray that they will love You L-rd with all their heart, with all their soul and with all their mind, might and strength and love their neighbor as themselves. (Deuteronomy 6:5, Mark 12:30, Matthew 22:37-39) Just as Samuel was dedicated to You as a child, so I give my children back to You. I pray that my children will seek You, L-rd, and shall not lack any good thing. (Psalm 34:10) Teach them how to grow in wisdom and stature and favor with you and favor with all people. (Luke 2:52) B'shem Yeshua (In the name of Jesus)

BLESSING FOR WIFE

Avinu Malkeinu (Our Father and King)

I thank you for my wife. I honor her. She is more precious to me than all the wealth in this world. I trust her with my whole heart. Bless her with strength and resourcefulness as she cares for our family. Bless her that she may hear our children rise up and call her blessed as she trusts in you and walks in the fear of the L-rd. Pour out your blessings upon her. Reward her with all the things she deserves. (Proverbs 31:10-31) B'shem Yeshua (In the name of Jesus)

BLESSING FOR HUSBAND

Avinu Malkeinu (Our Father and King)

I thank you for my husband. His trust is firmly in You. Because of You, he is steady in the storms of life. He is strong and courageous. He is a man of integrity who always seeks to do what is righteous. My heart is drawn to his kindness and compassion for others. He leads and loves our family well. He is honored among men and makes wise decisions. Give him increase in all he does (Psalm 112:1-9). B'shem Yeshua (In the name of Jesus)

Here are some traditional blessings that have been said:

When praying for the wife the husband can read from **Proverbs 31**

An accomplished woman who can find?
Her value is far beyond rubies.
Her husband's heart trusts in her,
and he lacks nothing valuable.
She brings him good and not harm
all the days of her life.
She selects wool and flax
and her hands work willingly.
She is like merchant ships,
bringing her sustenance from afar.
She rises while it is still night
and provides food for her household
and portions for her servant girls.
She considers a field and buys it.
From the fruit of her hands she plants a vineyard.
She girds herself with strength
and invigorates her arms.
She discerns that her business is good.
Her lamp never goes out at night.
She extends her hands to the spindle
and her palm grasps the spinning wheel.
She spreads out her palms to the poor,
and extends her hands to the needy.
She is not afraid of snow for her house,
for her whole household is clothed in scarlet wool.
She makes her own luxurious coverings.
Her clothing is fine linen and purple.
Her husband is respected at the city gates,
when he sits among the elders of the land.
She makes linen garments and sells them
and supplies sashes to the merchants.

Strength and dignity are her clothing,
and she laughs at the days to come.
She opens her mouth with wisdom—
a lesson of kindness is on her tongue.
She watches over the affairs of her household,
and does not eat the bread of idleness.
Her children arise and bless her,
her husband also praises her:
"Many daughters have excelled,
but you surpass them all."
Charm is deceitful and beauty is vain,
but a woman who fears Adonai will be praised.
Give her the fruit of her hands.
Let her deeds be her praise at the gates.

May you *(insert wife's name)* be blessed as you rise while it is yet night to see about the ways of our household and may you be blessed as you see about the daily care and education of our children. May your mouth be filled with wisdom and kindness.

A traditional blessing over the sons of the home

יברכך יהוה וישמרך יאר יהוה פניו אליך ויחנך ישא יהוה פניו אליך
וישם לך שלום

Y'varehc'cha Adonai v'yishm'recha, Ya'ayr Adonai panav 'aylecha v'yichunecha, Yisa' Adonai panav'aylecha v'yasem l'cha, shalom!

May the L-rd bless you and keep you. May he cause His face to shine upon you. May He lift His countenance upon you and give you peace. (Numbers 6:24-26)

Mother: May the L-rd fulfill our Sabbath prayer for you. May G-d make you good husbands and fathers.

Father: May He prepare and send holy wives for you. May the L-rd protect and defend you. May His Spirit fill you with grace.

May our family grow in happiness, please hear our Shabbat prayer, Amen.

A Traditional blessing over the daughters of the home

יברכך יהוה וישמרך יאר יהוה פניו אליך ויחנך ישא יהוה פניו אליך
וישם לך שלום

Y'varehc'cha Adonai v'yishm'recha, Ya'ayr Adonai panav 'aylecha v'yichunecha, Yisa' Adonai panav'aylecha v'yasem l'cha, shalom!

May the L-rd bless you and keep you. May he cause His face to shine upon you. May He lift up His countenance upon you and give you peace.

Mother: May the L-rd fulfill our Sabbath prayer for you. May G-d make you good mothers and wives.

Father: May He bring you a husband who will love, cherish, and care for you. May the L-rd protect and defend you. May His Spirit fill you with grace. May our family grow in happiness, please hear our Shabbat prayer, Amen.

Traditional Blessings over Husbands:

Wife/women: L-rd, thank you for giving me a husband.

Psalm 1:1-6

Happy is the one who has not walked in the advice of the wicked,
nor stood in the way of sinners,
nor sat in the seat of scoffers.
But his delight is in the Torah of Adonai,
and on His Torah he meditates day and night.
He will be like a planted tree over streams of water,
producing its fruit during its season.
Its leaf never droops—
but in all he does, he succeeds.
The wicked are not so.

For they are like chaff that the wind blows away.
Therefore the wicked will not stand during the judgment,
nor sinners in the congregation of the righteous.
For Adonai knows the way of the righteous,
but the way of the wicked leads to ruin.

May you (insert husband's name) be blessed as you rise and as you labor for the good of our household. And may you be blessed as you lead our family in the ways of the L-rd. May you mouth be filled with wisdom and kindness.[4]

Jeff Friedlander

RESTORING SACRED REST

Rest. What a concept. I am sure many of you may be familiar with modern science's discoveries of the power of rest. We now know the terrific benefits derived from even a short power nap.

As wonderful as it is that science confirms the power of rest, G-d knew this before we did. He designed our bodies system with a need for rest. He designed the proper amount needed and even designated the time to take it. What a great G-d we serve.

In ancient cultures, rest as a command would have been very unusual. Ancient cultures believed in work from dawn to dark every day. They would never have considered a thing such as rest. Then along comes the Hebrew people. They not only believe in rest but one full day every seven days. Not just on any day but on the seventh day. This was a revolutionary idea. Today we may see this as commonplace or even silly to consider as a big idea, however, in the ancient lands of the east, a day of rest was unthinkable.

G-d instructs us that on the seventh day we shall rest. This includes our animals, servants and foreigners living among us. Men, women, children, slaves, free, Jew, and Gentile were all commanded to rest (Exodus 20:8-11)[1] Here is an interesting thing I have discovered over the many years I have been practicing, teaching, and talking about Shabbat. People resist commands unless they foresee personal benefit. Our basic instinct doesn't like to be told what to do.

One of the most asked questions is why should we take or even more "obey" a command to have a sabbath? The minute I use the word 'command' people become nervous or even disagreeable.

However, if I commanded you to take a pay raise today with your job, would you be disagreeable? What if I commanded you to take your spouse out for a date and I would pay for everything? Would that also make you nervous? When we are commanded to do something, we want it to be obviously beneficial. Given benefit, we have no trouble accepting the command. However, when we are told to do something new or not on our list of "to do's", then we seem to struggle. When it comes to Shabbat, we like to take control and say we agree with the idea of rest, but we are to be the ones who determine the time and place.

And yet G-d commands us to take the seventh day and do something that all of us know, including the scientist and doctors, is good for us. We are commanded to rest. Why won't you?

A SHABBAT DRIVEN LIFE

The word translated as "rest" in Genesis 2:1-3 is used twice but has two different verb tenses. (Hebrew, like other languages, has grammar rules including those for verbs with different tenses which help us determine meaning.) The first use of the word "rest" or וַיִּשְׁבֹּת (way·yiš·bōṯ) is translated as "and He rested", giving us an indication that this was a past tense action. However, the verb tense in Hebrew would indicate this action was incomplete. The second time the word is used the verb tense indicates a completed action. What we can glean from this is that G-d himself is complete in His seventh day rest, but this is a rest which He is sequentially moving into the future. At times in the future, we will be able to participate in this rest.

The implications of this are immense. In the New Testament we read in Hebrews 4 the desire of the author for us to seek the rest promised by knowing G-d through the son, Yeshua. This rest is a Greek word: κατάπαυσις (katapausis). According to Thayer's

Greek Lexicon this word means actively putting to rest, as in a calming of the winds, and is used metaphorically here in Hebrews as "The heavenly blessedness in which G-d dwells, and of which he has promised to make persevering believers in Messiah partakers after the toils and trials of life on earth are ended:" [2]

The blessing of rest in heaven with G-d is complete--yet it also awaits us and thus is incomplete. This is the rest which G-d began in Genesis on the seventh day of creation. In Him, that rest is simultaneously complete and continual. It is sequential, yet cumulative and unending. That rest only comes as we make Yeshua our L-rd and submit fully to Yehovah. The writer of Hebrews communicates in the strongest possible way for each of us to "strive" so that we do not miss this rest.

Hebrews 4:9-13

*So then, there remains a Sabbath (sabbatismos in Greek) rest for the people of G-d, for whoever has entered G-d's rest (**katapausis**) has also rested from his works as G-d did from his.*

*Let us therefore **strive** to enter that rest, so that no one may fall by the same sort of disobedience. For the word of G-d is living and active, sharper than any two-edged sword, piercing to the division of soul and of spirit, of joints and of marrow, and discerning the thoughts and intentions of the heart. And no creature is hidden from his sight, but all are naked and exposed to the eyes of him to whom we must give account.*

G-d desires us to enter the Shabbat that He created and requires that we do this actively. The word translated "strive" means to "exert oneself, endeavor or give difference." We must be diligent about this and not allow a moment of time to get by where we do not engage in G-d's Shabbat.

Why is Shabbat so important?

The pinnacle of the creation week was reached as G-d rested and saw His creation as very good. He was in harmony with that which He had created. This is the ultimate goal of G-d toward humanity. There is no greater call of the Bible than this because it fulfills the single-minded purpose of scripture: G-d and His creation in harmonious coexistent rest, in the garden that He created. This is the place to which G-d wants us to return. This puts into perspective the "outcome of our faith, the salvation of our souls."[3]

What is Shabbat driven living?

Shabbat driven living means living Shabbat in a practical sense each week, on the seventh day as commanded, and living Shabbat each moment for all of eternity in the garden of "pleasure" Eden. This is the hope of mankind.

Shabbat is an appointed time both now and forever. The Hebrew word *mô'ēd* מוֹעֵד means appointed time and is also translated as congregation and assembly. The several "holidays" or *moadim* מוֹעֲדֵי of Leviticus 23 are among the most important days, seasons and times listed in the Bible. This word *moed* also means "to rehearse." These "days" are rehearsals in which we not only remember what G-d has done but also prepare for what He is going to do. This word then is translated as congregation, assembly, appointed time and rehearsal. When taken together we get a composite picture that tells us G-d's expectation of response to His holy days. We are to be as one in these. We must be unified in the honoring of these appointed times and as an assembly we must rehearse these each time the Biblical calendar calls for us to.

The first listed *moed* of Leviticus 23 is Shabbat. We must rehearse this great day each week in preparation for the eternal Shabbat that awaits.

Rather than ask "Why take a Shabbat?", the better question may be:

Why *not* take a Shabbat?

A command to rest is a glorious gift and one for which we should thank G-d rather than rebel. First, I believe if you struggle with this command then maybe you struggle to believe that G-d is good. Maybe you need to reevaluate your presuppositions or resistance to accepting His Plan: G-d gives commands for our benefit.[4] I am certain of this. G-d is good, and His commands are good for us. We should therefore never hesitate to hear and obey the commands of G-d.

People are busier than ever and survey after survey confirms that people are unhappy and unsatisfied with their quality of life. People work more hours and labor for more money. They look for satisfaction in entertainment and recreation, in sports and hobbies, in alcohol and drugs. You name it and we are attempting to find a way to scratch the itch of dissatisfaction. With all our activity and movement, one would think that an increased satisfaction in life would be the outcome. However, we find that people are not only less happy than in years past, but they are much more tired and using their time in ways that provide no real joy or long-lasting fruit. People commonly choose to rest by taking vacations, weekends, holidays, or days off work. Have you ever needed a vacation from your vacation? Sometimes our time off is more tiring and stressful than our time on. The Shabbat is not like that. The Shabbat is a time when G-d refreshes the soul in a way that only He can.

This is the time from the beginning that G-d himself set aside and then commanded His people to follow in His way. So, when we choose to follow this command to rest on the seventh day something supernatural happens. We are in the appointed time of rest and G-d supplies what we need in a supernatural way.

What are rest and work?

We tend to define rest by saying that it is the absence of work. Then we work to define work.

People ask if particular tasks are considered work on Shabbat. For example, one person asked if grocery shopping was acceptable on Shabbat. Another asked if cutting the grass was okay. Still another asked if they could do a onetime side job on Shabbat to make a little extra money. Several have asked me if they are allowed to go out to a park or to some entertainment venue on Shabbat and enjoy an event. Finally, some have asked if they must leave a job that requires them to work on Saturday, in order not to be sinning against G-d.

These questions are legitimate and good. In fact, I would say they are the questions asked by most people who love G-d and want to honor His word. So many people desire to obey G-d and desire to honor Shabbat, but their current lifestyle does not line up with G-d's revelations about Shabbat. This results in conflicted souls.

Let's answer the general inquiry before the specific examples. My normal answer to people when they ask these kinds of questions is simple. "I am not your Pharisee." My tongue and cheek response are designed to communicate a truth I believe in. As a trained messianic Rabbi, a teacher, a Christian trained Pastor, and a leader of a local community of followers of Messiah Yeshua, I can say without reservation that people want someone to tell them what is allowed, and I do not want to tell what is allowed in an area that is broad and deep.

Yeshua faced the Pharisees down on many issues because they created rules and regulations to follow that were not listed in the Torah. To be fair, they were in some ways reacting to historical circumstances. When Israel was exiled to Babylon and then returned to the land by a miracle of G-d's deliverance, they wanted to do right. They began to build "fences" around the Torah. In other words, they realized that they had been exiled because of disobedience and when they returned, discovered, and read the Torah they were "cut to the heart," and wept aloud. They were sorrowful because they knew they had been rebellious and disobedient. For that reason, they responded by beginning to pass down oral commands they claimed were from G-d, intended to create Torah obedience. The truth is we do not have any way to verify these "oral commands." Many of these continued to be passed down and eventually were written down as the "oral law." Thus, a system of fences was created to keep the people from sinning against G-d. These fences added many words and rules to the written Torah commands, and it became impossible for the people to keep all of these.

Yeshua challenged the Pharisees on these rulings on many occasions. I suggest He would make the same challenges to us today. In this book we cover several of these passages where Yeshua argues his position on the definition of work and rest as related to Shabbat. For now, we will simply say that each person must seek G-d in defining personal rest.

This law of Rest is Hard, right?

A comment that signals the truth of the heart of many is that the "law" is hard or impossible to keep. The suggestion, stated or unstated, is that G-d created something that we are unable to understand much less abide in. Let's take a closer look at this presumption.

Deuteronomy 30:10-14

-when you obey the voice of the L-rd your G-d, to keep his commandments and his statutes that are written in this Book of the Law, when you turn to the L-rd your G-d with all your heart and with all your soul.

"For this commandment that I command you today is not too hard for you, neither is it far off. It is not in heaven, that you should say, 'Who will ascend to heaven for us and bring it to us, that we may hear it and do it?' Neither is it beyond the sea, that you should say, 'Who will go over the sea for us and bring it to us, that we may hear it and do it?' But the word is very near you. It is in your mouth and in your heart, so that you can do it."

The passage tells us plainly that the commandment is not in a place that cannot be found, but rather is very near to us, even in our mouth and heart. For what purpose? "So that you can do it."

The key to this is v10." ... when you turn to the L-rd your G-d with all your heart and with all your soul." Obeying the commands of G-d are always connected to the heart of the follower. Our behaviors will follow our hearts desire. The mind will justify what the heart wants. Thus, obeying the commands of G-d, both the 'do's and don'ts,' is not hard when our hearts are fully devoted to our G-d.

Ezekiel the prophet of G-d promises the following:

Ezekiel 36:24-28

For I will take you from the nations, gather you out of all the countries and bring you back to your own land. Then I will sprinkle clean water on you and you will be clean from all your uncleanness and from all your idols. Moreover I will give you a new heart. I will put a new spirit within you. I will remove the stony heart from your flesh and give you a heart of flesh. I will put My Ruach within you. Then I will cause you to walk in My laws, so you will keep My rulings and do them. Then you will live in the land that I gave to your fathers. You will be My people and I will be your God.

This is the statement of the Bible, not a man-made commentary. G-d says when He puts His Spirit in you it will cause you to walk in His laws and those laws are in your mouth and heart.

In **Romans 10:4-9**, Rabbi Shaul brings us a more expanded understanding of this phrase.

For the goal at which the Torah aims is the Messiah, who offers righteousness to everyone who trusts. For Moshe writes about the righteousness grounded in the Torah that the person who does these things will attain life through them. Moreover, the righteousness grounded in trusting says:

"Do not say in your heart, 'Who will ascend to heaven?'"—

that is, to bring the Messiah down—or, "'Who will descend into Sh'ol?'"—that is, to bring the Messiah up from the dead. What, then, does it say?

"The word is near you, in your mouth and in your heart."—that is, the word about trust which we proclaim, namely, that if you acknowledge publicly with your mouth that Yeshua is L-rd and trust in your heart that G-d raised him from the dead, you will be delivered.

Notice, Paul does not change the words of Deuteronomy but echoes them. He simply explains that for this law to be in your heart and mouth it comes from the relationship that is built in faith in Yeshua.

One cannot have the law written on his heart without faith.

Hebrews 11:6 states that,

Now without faith it is impossible to please G-d for those that come to him must believe that He exist and that He is a rewarder of those who believe or trust.

Jeremiah 31:32

But this is the covenant I will make with the house of Israel after those days"—it is a declaration of Adonai—I will put My Torah within them. Yes, I will write it on their heart. I will be their God and they will be My people.

Ultimately, then, we can conclude that Yeshua is the fulfillment of the promise of Deuteronomy. The law is not too hard to do, understand or to receive if you are born again and filled with the Spirit of G-d. For those that are truly born again the law becomes a natural way to live and obedience to the law is a desire born out of the heart. The spirit gives us a life that intellectual or willful obedience to the letter of the law cannot give. The letter kills because it is not the heart of G-d but rather the external behavior of man. Each time man tries to obey G-d's true law found in Torah without the Spirit of G-d enabling him, he will not only fail but will try to figure out a way to make it attainable to follow.

But the Spirit requires us to submit our lives to G-d. The Spirit requires us to pray and listen to G-d for understanding and wisdom. The Spirit requires us to be willing to serve G-d rather than the culture around us and most certainly more than rules we contrive for ourselves. G-d has given us a playbook and He is the owner of the team. We do not have the right to change the playbook by adding to it or taking away from it.

To Shabbat is to Renew

Jeremiah 31:31-34

"Behold, the days are coming, declares the L-rd, when I will make a new covenant with the house of Israel and the house of Judah, not like the covenant that I made with their fathers on the day when I took them by the hand to bring them out of the land of Egypt, my covenant that they broke, though I was their husband, declares the L-rd. For this is the covenant that I will make with the house of Israel after those days, declares the L-rd: I will put my law within them, and I will write it on their hearts. And I will be their G-d, and they shall be my people. And no longer shall each one teach his neighbor and each his brother, saying, 'Know the L-rd,' for they shall all know me, from the least of them to the greatest, declares the L-rd. For I will forgive their iniquity, and I will remember their sin no more."

Here we see the promise of the New Covenant. It does not replace or remove the previous covenants but rather builds upon them. This then is what Yeshua was talking about when we read the following:

Luke 22:19-20

And he took bread, and when he had given thanks, he broke it and gave it to them, saying, "This is my body, which is given for you. Do this in remembrance of me." And likewise, the cup after they had eaten, saying, "This cup that is poured out for you is the new covenant in my blood."

This covenant of body and blood is the open door that we walk through by faith. In doing so, we become the children of Abraham and part of the covenant promised in Jeremiah to Judah and Israel. To be a part of Israel is to be spiritually grafted into the tree of life that is provided by G-d through His son. This tree is nourished by the Jewish root according to Paul. Romans 11:13-24. Thus, to be "born again" is not to remove ourselves from the covenants G-d has given to Israel but rather to embrace them. These covenants are our gift and legacy to pass on.

This new covenant is powerful because this is what we do each week. The Hebrew picture of Shabbat from the roots, which are the nourishment of the "olive tree" can be summed up in this idea. Each Shabbat we are renewing our covenant relationship with G-d through the son.

To Shabbat is to Reset

We get to have a reset button hit each week which gives us a fresh start. Each of us that use a computer can understand this. As you use your computer the memory and programs begin to store information. This information builds up over time in a cache file. A short-term file that can be used to access frequently used data quickly.

The simplest solution is to shut everything you are working on down and restart the computer. This stopping of work and reset of the computer gives it a fresh start. The cache is cleaned out and the computer begins to work properly.

We are not computers, but we work the same way. Our cache gets full, and each week and we must turn off and restart. Shabbat gives us the reset button and freshens up the machine. G-d knew how he designed us and that if we obeyed him, renewed the covenant, and reset the system through rest each week then we would be more joyful and effective.

The Tech Thief and Digital Distractions

Many today are suffering from sleep deprivation. A new study has found a lack of sleep among the U.S. workforce costs approximately $411 billion and 1.2 million working days per year, [1]

The Bureau of Labor Statistics' 2016 American Time Use Survey revealed that people are increasingly taking their work home with them. The average American does 4.5 hours of work at home each week, and 20 percent spend 10 hours or more. In the UK, a survey of managers found that this after-hours work time was enough to equal or exceed their annual leave.[2]

Did you know according to the *Centers for Disease Control & Prevention,* nearly one-third of American working adults (about 41 million people) get less than 6 hours of sleep per night?

It has been said that time is the greatest resource we have because it is the one resource we can never get back. Each minute of our day is a minute that is unrecoverable—never to be used again. This renders time a depreciating asset and increases its value.

So, I ask you, where does your time go? Are you too busy to live? Does life seem to be delivering much less than you expected? Are you so busy that even planning a vacation is stressful?

Study after study confirms that our modern society suffers from sleep deprivation, depression, and dissatisfaction with life. The hustle and bustle of life impacts productivity and our health.

Invisible Enemy

This condition is not random but a planned strategy of an enemy of our souls.

We are at war with an unseen enemy, and many have fallen prey to the strategically orchestrated great deception of distraction. You may not see the wind, but you certainly feel the effects. Our society feels the effects of this deception as well.

The Bible refers to this power as the devil or the Satan. His strategy from the beginning was to cause man to question the ways of G-d. He revealed this tactic when he asked Eve, "Did G-d really say…?" He has been asking that same question generation after generation to distract us from the truth in G-d's word. His second tactic is to get us to engage the blame game. When confronted by G-d about eating the forbidden fruit we hear Adam blame Eve, then Eve blames the serpent who was then cursed by G-d. The enemy employs this strategy from generation to generation.

Many dismiss the source of attack. They link this war to society generally. They blame everything from Hollywood to McDonalds. They believe the world is out to get them and they have no recourse or power because they are the little people and as the saying goes, "You can't fight city hall."

The blame is pushed on the government, parents, or the circumstances of life. We become victims of the people around us, and the poor fruit of our life is the fault of another.

No matter what your belief is concerning the source of the deception you can be assured the attack is real and the destruction is fast and furious. Do you still wonder, "What attack are you talking about?"

The attack on you! You must recognize you have been targeted to be taken out of an effective life reflecting eternal value. The enemy of our soul is an unseen power, sending out tactical armament against humanity in order to disrupt and destroy our faith.

This unseen enemy hates us and desires us to be ineffective. The enemy persuades us to hate ourselves and thereby view creation and G-d from ambivalent or distorted lenses. In opposite fashion, he puffs us up to love ourselves so much that we elevate our desires above G-d and sacrifice relationships for self-preservation. Either maneuver is an assault on the order of G-d.

The Satan has learned something over his thousands of years of watching and afflicting people: People will do anything to please themselves. He will use whatever he can to make us more selfish and self-sustaining. His desire is for us to believe that we are not in need of any help, especially divine aid. He devises scenarios convincing us of independence from G-d and one another, and therefore the fruit of our lives reflects this depravity.

Distractions are a strategy.

One strategy we are seeing in our society is the deception of distractions.

These can take the form of good/positive distractions or bad/evil distractions. Good distractions embody charitable work, spending time with friends or family or maybe pursuing some entertainment or physical activity. The deception begins when we allow our hobbies, our relationships, our giving to become the larger priority of our life, thus distractions push us from keeping G-d at the center of life, activities, and relationships.

Evil distractions are easily discernable. **Galatians 5:18** contains an excellent summary of evil distractions:

Now the deeds of the flesh are clear: sexual immorality, impurity, indecency, idolatry, witchcraft, hostility, strife, jealousy, rage, selfish ambition, dissension, factions, envy, drunkenness, carousing, and things like.

Indulging in these Biblically defined evils replaces G-d as the sovereign over our affairs with these distractions.

There are distractions that can seem neutral, such as television. Watching a favorite movie or tv show can be an encouragement and uplifting. However, when T.V. viewing becomes "binge watching" this may cross the line into evil distractions. We must use discernment to maintain a healthy balance.

Once time is spent, it cannot be recovered. Balancing the distractions is accomplished only when we keep G-d in the very center of the dial of our life. We must allow G-d to allot our daily time.

Psalm 16:9

The heart of man plans his course,

but Adonai directs his steps.

We are created in the image of G-d and therefore are designed to be creative with the gifts G-d has weaved into the fabric our being. The distractions of this world keep us busy and always racing against time to complete the next task. This pace convinces us that taking a day of rest on Shabbat would be a waste of time.

This explains one of the reasons people fail to take a Shabbat. The speed to which our lives has become accustomed prevents us from resting. We live in a culture that moves so fast with technology that we have become addicted to the habit of a quick fix. The idea of taking a twenty-four hour period with the purpose of rest, renewal and relationship feels unattainable and unproductive.

Technology Thief

John 10:10

The thief comes only to steal, slaughter, and destroy. I have come that they might have life and have it abundantly!

Our enemy is characterized as a thief. John reminds us that the plan of this thief is to leave us utterly destroyed.

One tool at the disposal of the enemy is electricity.

Imagine for a moment the world without electricity. Imagine no TV to entertain us, no phones to connect us, no computers to work on, and no cars to transport us, just to name a few of the convenience's electricity brings. These modern comforts are certainly not evil, but we can be deceived by our dependance on them.

What did we do before these technological advances came into our lives? We actually talked to each other. We were more dependent on community life. We needed interactions with people to live. Today, we allow technology to rob us of these vital interactions.

Now before you assume that I am crazy and believe all computers are evil and that cell phones are from Satan, let me clarify. I am not anti-technology, nor do I believe that the high-tech world and advancements are the death of us. However, I am certain that we are currently on a track to lose authentic and genuine relationships.

Steve Jobs, founder of Apple and incidentally one of the wealthiest men in the world, said this prior to his death: "Remembering that I'll be dead soon is the most important tool I've ever encountered to help me make the big choices in life. Because almost everything - all external expectations, all pride, all fear of embarrassment or failure - these things just fall away in the face of death, leaving only what is truly important."

Ultimately, we came into this world with nothing, and we will leave with nothing but the legacy of the relationships into which we engaged and invested.

Matthew 22:37-39

And He (Yeshua) said to him, "'You shall love ADONAI your G-d with all your heart, and with all your soul, and with all your mind.' This is the first and greatest commandment. And the second is like it, 'You shall love your neighbor as yourself.'

Technology has become a tool many people feel they cannot live without. Whether texting, calling or internet surfing, or a night of Netflix binge watching, we are consumed with entertainment, news, and social media sound bites. Matthew reminds us that our proper priorities are first, G-d, and second, true human interaction. These values constitute the two most important commandments, according to Yeshua, quoting the Tanakh (Old Testament.)

Technology has afforded us the gift of speed and efficiency wrapped in the deception of the loss of interpersonal time.

We can go online to buy homes, stocks, groceries and even gifts for holidays. We do not have to interact with a single human being to take care of the necessities of life. Prior to these technological advances, we spoke to a realtor to buy a home or a stockbroker to secure a portfolio; we interacted with the local grocer and department store clerk. We ran into friends while shopping and caught up with one another's lives.

Today, we maximize our time and go online to shop saving time and even money. We do not see the product until it arrives via shipping. We do not interact with a human and our society dangerously embraces this way of life that isolates us from each other.

We even see this in our religious communities. The technology thief has infiltrated our religious experience. It is fashionable now to watch services online rather than be hassled with in person attendance.

I remember when congregations met several times a week. We invested time into our spiritual relationships and in learning from our spiritual leaders. We built relationships with people around the Bible and our faith, rather than around likes and dislikes on a social media platform.

Today, religious services are neatly packaged: an orderly message; structured worship time; online availability. We have been robbed of the joy of human interaction in the context of our spiritual community. Sadly, many houses of worship are working extra hard to make attendance through the internet easier than ever. Using technology to its fullest degree, the body of Messiah sacrifices meaningful connections for efficiency and incipient laziness. (After all, church in pjs is easier than breakfast, dressing, and gathering children to head out by 8:43 AM for 9:00 AM church). We have forgotten G-d's timely words from **Genesis 2:18** *"It is not good that man is alone."*

We have been blinded to the idea that spiritual relationships with one another are central to our life on earth. In fact, Yeshua said our spiritual and loving relationships with each other are equal to our loving relationship with G-d. Loving people is not possible in isolation. Loving people most certainly is not neatly ordered! It is only possible when measured in time. (I originally wrote this section several years ago and as I edit this book, we are in the middle of the pandemic of Covid-19.) Isolation and technology-thievery are real, and the bad fruit is beginning to ripen.

I have been married to my wife since 1990. I can say without hesitation that in sharing three decades of history, we must spend quality, non-ministry time together. Neither of us, nor the marriage, could survive a texting relationship or facetime communication exclusively. Neglecting time with each other fosters cracks in the relationship and may communicate lack of love. Love is time.

The technology enhancements of the last quarter century have been incredible, and I enjoy using these in my own life. However, we must ask ourselves;

- What is the cost? Is the quality of your conversations with those you love increasing in quality and quantity or decreasing?
- Do you spend more time mindlessly scrolling social media rather than connecting personally with others?
- Is it hard to go to sleep at night without looking at your phone?
- Do you dedicate as much time to face to face conversations as your tweets, texts, emails, and social media posts?

These technologies are not evil but can easily become distractions. We can become deceived into believing that we are more connected than previously by the number of "likes" and comments on our posts. This is not a genuine human connection but a poor substitute for self-love.

The Art of Communication

"Although we send information faster and more often than at any time in history, we have let technology replace authentic communication."[3]

We hide behind our computer screens and exercise our "keyboard courage." We are losing the ability to thoughtfully communicate with one another. Much communication is watered down to a quick sentence or emoji.

"One of the skills of communication is to **read the nonverbal cues of the speaker.** Authentic communication goes beyond information transfer and into relationship building. For instance, it is a skill to know how to successfully navigate a tense situation in conflict resolution." [4]

We cannot discern these cues hiding behind a screen and keyboard.

Human interaction has been replaced with an email, text, or social media post. We express ourselves using our devices rather than our interpersonal skills. Interpersonal skills are developed as we spend time with each other. We learn how to interact with each other in a civil and loving manner. We have moved into a realm of electronic communication exclusively. We can talk to friends and colleagues from our living rooms and never see them personally.

The Cost of Entertainment

Another area the technology thief has infiltrated is entertainment. We used to go to entertainment venues with people but now it is so easy to just sit at home alone and watch the expansive collection of movies and entertainment options available at the touch of a button. We are entertained in isolation and robbed of a collective experience with others. We can literally turn our brains off and allow others to think for us. We turn on the TV and "veg out" for several hours. With the advent of "binge watching" through internet services people have submitted to brainwashing. We allow producers, directors, and actors to define and paint our pictures of life.

The original format of television programming was a forty-five-minute episode per week, interrupted with commercials. The weeklong break between episodes gave space for the individual imagination to explore the possible scenarios of the next episode. Binge watching without commercials for hours on end, day after day creates a blur between reality and fiction. We allow these programs to shape our understanding of life and relationships. We are robbed of the ability to measure truth against lies and reality against fantasy. These programs train our next generation on conflict resolution, parental and delegated authority, and moral and ethical philosophies apart from the Word of G-d. [5,6]

We have hurt ourselves by missing the best part of life; the satisfaction of truly connecting with another human being. When you look into another's eyes while talking and listening, you and the other person have related at the level of the soul.

Matthew 6:2

The eye is the lamp of the body. You draw light into your body through your eyes, and light shines out to the world through your eyes. So, if your eye is well and shows you what is true, then your whole body will be filled with light.

Technology robs us of this priceless encounter. These intangible moments are undiscernible when we are stationed behind our monitors. The eyes are the gateway to the soul. Relationships are more than just knowing about someone through information transfer but rather we know someone on a deeper level when we can look into their eyes to see their hurts and joys and then respond appropriately.

I remember sitting with my wife recently and looking at her. I saw her eyes and thought that I am the most fortunate man on earth. She looked back at me, and it felt for a moment as though we were back in college and had just met and fallen in love. We connected!

Technology robs these moments. Selah.

All of this can seem a bit depressing. Well, I am sorry for the discouraging words of reality, but we must be honest in our evaluation of ourselves and our culture if we are to grow as disciples. The good news is G-d's word has a solution.

Shabbat. Yes, simple, and elegant. Shabbat is a powerful key to correcting the problems technology birthed. Shabbat arrests the enemy and limits his exposure to our lives; without access, he cannot rob us of relationship joy.

Shabbat is a consistent, weekly, sacred time of rest. As you enter into Shabbat each week and disconnect from technology, G-d can begin to tear down these technologically produced walls and restore community and family back into their rightful place. Just by being present in Shabbat, you experience the joy of community and fellowship.

The power of a full day of rest without the constant "need" to connect through tech may at first be very difficult, however, as the weeks go on you will find yourself craving the "rest" of Shabbat. This craving will grow and over time you will notice a longing for the day of rest. More than that your productive work week will become more productive as the "time wasters" will become less interesting to you. G-d will supernaturally realign your priorities and your thoughts. Distractions will no longer be negative. They will now become intentional moments of life that are built into the fabric of your soul. G-d uses this amazing command to rest to change your life.

Jeff Friedlander

WHAT IS WORK?

A common question that arises when one is embracing the Shabbat rest is "What constitutes rest?" People want a list dictating which activities are "okay" and which are deemed "work?"

This is a fantastic question and one that scholars have wrestled with through the generations.

In this chapter, we explore definitions of work according to Jewish authorities and according to the written word itself. In the next chapter we will use the Bible to define what we can specifically "do and not do" according to the word of G-d on Shabbat. We see benefits that have come from guarding and keeping the Shabbat. G-d's ways are not our ways, and His ways are higher than our ways;[1] when we follow them, we receive the joy and shalom of His life flowing through us.

WORK

In modern society, the five-day work week with two days off for the weekend guides most of our lives. The model came into practice in 1908. A New England cotton mill was the first American factory to move to a five-day work week. The Jewish workers didn't want to work on Shabbat, but the hours were required to be made up on Sunday. The Christian workers found this to be unfair so the mill closed on Saturday and Sunday so both faiths could practice their day of rest. In 1926, Henry Ford adopted this schedule for his factory workers and other industries caught on and it became a standard to work a five-day work week.[2]

Today, many European companies are even considering shortening the work week to four days. G-d ordained that we should work six days and rest on the seventh; we shall see the unfolding repercussions as man again redefines G-d's Word.

WHAT IS WORK ACCORDING TO ORTHODOX RABBIS?

In modern America, we take the five-day workweek so much for granted that we forget what a radical concept a day of rest was in ancient times. The weekly day of rest has no parallel in any other ancient civilization. In ancient times, leisure was for the wealthy and the ruling classes only, never for the serving or laboring classes. In addition, the very idea of rest each week was unimaginable. The Greeks thought Jews were lazy because we insisted on having a "holiday" every seventh day.

Rabbinical Orthodox Judaism has been one of the few faiths who have firmly defined and held Shabbat as a priority of practice. Due to their passion for Torah and desire to keep Shabbat, the Rabbis have created an extensive list of prohibitions. This to some degree has contributed to the confusion of Shabbat. What is allowed and what is not allowed. Before you read the next section, I want to say clearly that I am grateful and appreciative of my Jewish friends. Although we differ in our view of Shabbat and the work allowed, I respect and admire their heartfelt desire to guard the Shabbat as commanded.

The Hebrew word for work is מְלָאכָה, *melacha* first seen in

Genesis 2:2:

God completed—on the seventh day—His work that He made, and He ceased—on the seventh day—from all His work that He made.

Melaka means occupation, work, and business. Historical Shabbat restrictions are based on the Rabbinical understanding of connecting *melaka* to the act of creation. In addition, the

Rabbis have argued that this *melaka* extends to include the work of building the tabernacle. Exodus 31:12-18 is the admonition Moses gave to Israel, including honoring Shabbat. This speech was given in the midst of giving the instructions for building the tabernacle, leading the Rabbis to conclude that Shabbat rest directly relates to resting from the work of building the tabernacle. Jewish law, as taken from Torah, Talmud, and Mishnah, would define the Hebrew word *melaka* as related to the act of being creative or doing creative activities such as problem solving. Also, they interpret this word as exercising control over your environment.

How did the Rabbi's come to this conclusion?

The Rabbis state that this word is rarely used outside of the context of creation and tabernacle/temple work. For example, Chabad describes the two words of work this way:

"The Hebrew language has two words for "work"--*avodah* and *melaka*. *Avodah* is a general term meaning work, while *melaka* has a very precise *halachic* meaning. On Shabbat, *melaka* is prohibited. Our Sages explain that *melaka* refers to the activities which were necessary for construction of the *Mishkan*, the traveling sanctuary which the Jews took with them throughout their desert wanderings.

The Torah specifically mentions two *melachot*, kindling a fire and carrying wood. The Mishnah further explains that 39 different categories of *melaka* went into building the *Mishkan (tabernacle)*. While these categories of labor refer to the construction of the *Mishkan*, they actually encompass all forms of human productivity." [3]

For those unfamiliar with this, to have a *halachic* (the way) meaning is to have an interpreted meaning given from the rabbis and carrying the weight of law. Simply put, a halachic ruling is Jewish law. The rabbis define what is "work" and one must adhere to their definition, or you are sinning against G-d himself.

Using this method, they conclude that any activity which could be placed in a category of creative work or was work that was used in the building of the tabernacle or temple must be restricted on Shabbat.

Wikipedia provides some further explanation of the way in which Jewish law has, since the first century, added to the written word.

> "*Halakha* (Jewish law), especially the Talmud tractate Shabbat, identifies thirty-nine categories of activity prohibited on Shabbat (Hebrew: ל"ט אבות מלאכות, *lamed tet avot melakhot*), and clarifies many questions surrounding the application of the Biblical prohibitions. Many of these activities are also prohibited on the Jewish holidays listed in the Torah, although there are significant exceptions permitting carrying and preparing food under specific circumstances."

> "The thirty-nine *melakhot* are *categories* of activity. For example, while "winnowing" usually refers exclusively to the separation of chaff from grain, in the Talmudic sense it can refer to any separation of intermixed materials which renders edible that which was inedible. Thus, filtering undrinkable water to make it drinkable falls under this category, as does picking small bones from fish.

> Many rabbinic scholars have pointed out that these regulations of labor have something in common – they prohibit any activity that is *creative*, or that exercises control or dominion over one's *environment*." [4]

The Jewish authorities have concluded that there are many activities which must be restricted. Modern societal developments give them license to regulate more activities or provide enhanced applications. The reason the Rabbi's claim authority here is their belief in the "oral law." These laws purportedly were passed down from Moses to the tribal elders and so on and so on to today. When it comes to defining work on Shabbat, the Rabbis admit that their definitions are almost entirely from an oral tradition rather than the written words of Moses.

> "The way in which we determine what activities are prohibited on Shabbos requires some background. Only a handful of the 39 categories of prohibited activity on Shabbos are mentioned explicitly in the Torah. The Torah simply states: " The seventh day is Shabbos...don't do any "Melacha" " (Exodus 20:10). It is left up to the Oral Law, taught by G-d to Moses on Mount Sinai, to define precisely what activities are called "Melacha" and hence prohibited on Shabbos. The Oral Law (Mishna, Shabbos 7:2) lists 39 activities which are defined as "Melacha"; each of these 39 is called an "Av," which in its broadest sense means "prototype." Any activity which is similar to one of these 39 prototype activities, is called a "Toldah" ("derivative") and is also considered to be a "Melacha" prohibited by the Torah."[5]

The Rabbi's have assumed Biblical authority, placing additional rules on the people who follow this sect of Judaism.

DEFINING WORK ACCORDING TO THE WORD

In contrast to the Rabbinical definition of work, but with respect, I would like to offer a Biblical view from the written word itself.

The word מְלָאכָה *Melakah* is used repeatedly in the Bible and refers to people doing their normal "work or craft."

Genesis 39:11

And it came to pass about this time, that Joseph went into the house to do his business; (מְלָאכָה / Melakah) and there was none of the men of the house there within.

Proverbs 18:9

He also that is slothful in his work (מְלָאכָה / Melakah) is brother to him that is a great waster.

Proverbs 22:29

Seest thou a man diligent in his business? (מְלָאכָה / Melakah) he shall stand before kings; he shall not stand before men.

Jonah 1:8

Then they said to him, "Tell us, now! On whose account is this evil happening to us? What is your profession (מְלָאכָה / Melakah) and where did you come from? What is your land and from what nation are you?"

So, the word "work" should be more clearly looked at as the labor you normally pursue as a vocation or position. This is the Hebrew word to describe all aspects of work. One's vocation, profession. This interpretation clearly differs from Halakic law described above.

The Bible wisely does not articulate a list of the activities that are permitted and/or restricted on Shabbat. However, there are verses from which we can glean the wisdom the Bible offers. Within these verses we learn about some restrictions and the blessings that come with obedience.

WHAT CAN I DO ON SHABBAT?

In the last chapter we saw that the definition of work in the Bible normally means ones vocational work.

First, we must understand the text was written in an agricultural time in history; that context frames the principles.

Exodus 34:21

Six days you shall work, but on the seventh day you shall rest. In plowing time and in harvest you shall rest.

Vocationally, plowing and harvesting were work. We can think of this as "field labor." This understanding leads us to ask the question of ourselves, "What do we do for six days a week for our vocation?" What does a workday look like for us?

The Bible references this normal labor that we perform the other six days of the week. *Melakot's* Biblical definition encompasses vocational work. The following questions may help you determine how work is defined:

- Am I doing the same thing on Shabbat that I do on the other six days of the week?
- Am I earning money on Shabbat through work like I do the other six days of the week?
- Am I disengaging from my normal routine of creative work during this twenty-four-hour period from Friday night at sundown to Saturday night at sundown?

The scripture says that G-d wants to give the animals, the earth, the men, the women, the children, the servants, and the noncitizens of Israel a day of rest. Maybe a few examples would be useful here.

If I am a mechanic and take a Shabbat, I probably should not work on cars during Shabbat. If I am an accountant, then I should probably not do tax work on Shabbat. If I am a homemaker and stay at home during the week, then I should not take care of the house on Shabbat. What?

Here, the complexities of giving rules for every category of work becomes apparent. This is why I refuse to be "your Pharisee" and dictate your definition of work.

Obviously if you are a stay-at-home mom, Shabbat does not mean it is okay leave little Johnny in his room all day to fend for himself even though he is only two years old. G-d is not expecting that everything we do on a normal day will not be done on a Holy Day. We must feed ourselves, but maybe we have food prepared the day before to just be warmed up. We still must take care of our children and keep things safe. If a person is a medical, fire, police, or emergency worker they may have to work on Shabbat. If someone is having a heart attack, we certainly would not want the doctor to say, "I am sorry it is Shabbat, hang in there till tomorrow."

As Yeshua said, it is good to heal on the Shabbat. I do not believe in hard and fast rules that define "work" and "rest" for these reasons. Rather we should understand the heart of G-d and His desire to bless us with rest and call us into a special time of renewed covenant with Him.

But I can't quit my job and I must work on Shabbat!

For those that have jobs which require work on Shabbat, I suggest that you simply pray and seek G-d's guidance. G-d is gracious and wants you to succeed in your job and simultaneously wants to give you His Shabbat. But do not make the mistake of believing because your current job requires work on Shabbat that

G-d is not able or willing to provide a scheduling adjustment. He wants you to honor His word first and foremost.

Pray and ask G-d that He may give you a way to get the day off each week or even provide a new and better job. His ways are good and mysterious.

Remember, in Deuteronomy 6:23-25, G-d tells us that when our children ask why we are given the commands of the Torah and why we obey them we are to provide this answer:

He brought us out from there in order to bring us to the land he had sworn to our ancestors that he would give us. **Adonai ordered us to observe all these laws, to fear Adonai our G-d, always for our own good, so that he might keep us alive, as we are today.** *It will be righteousness for us if we are careful to obey all these mitzvot before Adonai our G-d, just as he ordered us to do.* (emphasis mine)

We follow the laws because they are always for our own good and through them He keeps us alive. These are as righteousness to us.

So, do not be afraid to ask for the Shabbat off from your job because G-d has given it to you as gift and He, not your job, is G-d.

Buying and Selling

Nehemiah 13:15-18

*At that time, I saw men in Judah **treading winepresses** on the sabbath, and others bringing heaps of grain and loading them onto asses, also wine, grapes, figs, and all sorts of goods, and bringing them into Jerusalem on the sabbath. I admonished them there and then for selling provisions. Tyrians who lived there brought fish and all sorts of wares and **sold them** on the sabbath to the Judahites in Jerusalem. I censured the nobles of Judah, saying to them, 'What evil thing is this that you are doing, profaning the sabbath day! This is just what your ancestors did,* *and for it G-d brought all this misfortune on this city; and now you give cause for further wrath against Israel by profaning the sabbath!'*

Here the Israelites have returned to Israel from Babylonian exile, and they begin to examine what the Torah commands as it relates to Shabbat. Their clear interpretation is that buying, selling, preparing goods for market is doing the same thing on Shabbat as they would do the other six days and it is rightfully considered a profane sin. They conclude that carelessness toward the law of G-d caused the exile. The question is asked, "Do you think G-d is going to allow us to do the same thing our ancestors did and escape punishment?"

From Genesis to Moses and now in the example of those returned from exile, the law of Shabbat is to not perform your normal work on Shabbat and to refrain from doing those things that prepare for your normal work, on the Sabbath.

Isaiah 58:13-14

If you turn back your foot from Shabbat,
from doing your pleasure on My holy day,
and call Shabbat a delight,
the holy day of Adonai honorable,
If you honor it, not going your own ways,
not seeking your own pleasure,
nor speaking your usual speech, then You will delight yourself in Adonai,
and I will let you ride over the heights of the earth,
I will feed you with the heritage of your father Jacob.
For the mouth of Adonai has spoken.

Isaiah reminds us of the great promise received when we delight in the Shabbat and keep it holy. He links the holiness and delight of Shabbat to resting from your normal work or personal affairs. Shabbat is the one day reserved for no transactions.

Carrying a Burden

Jeremiah 17:22

Nor shall you carry out burdens from your houses on the sabbath day, or do any work, but you shall hallow the sabbath day, as I commanded your fathers.

We should ask what G-d was communicating through Jeremiah regarding not carrying "burdens" from their homes on Shabbat? Jeremiah 17 must be read in the context of the previous chapter as well. Jeremiah is being used of the L-rd to rebuke the people for all the sins which had been described in **Jeremiah 16:18**

But first I will doubly repay their iniquity and their sin, because they have polluted my land with the carcasses of their detestable idols and have filled my inheritance with their abominations.

The ancestors of the Jewish people had possessed false g-ds and idols. It was this false religion that the people of Jeremiah's day were following. Through Jeremiah, G-d refers to the altars bowed down to as if they were gods, when they were not G-d.

When we get to verse 21 the prophet says, "take heed to yourselves" which literally means "in your souls" and then he says to bear no burden on the sabbath day and not to bring a burden to the gates of Jerusalem. This burden that is within the "soul" and that could be carried to the gate has a double meaning. First, it means the burdens of the soul. Carry not your worries and anxieties, carry not your pains but rather on Shabbat enter into mental and emotional rest. Remove intentionally all the cares of this world for this one day. Allow yourself to fully retreat from bearing the weight of the responsibilities and efforts of each day that you carry. Instead take this time of Shabbat and lay all of that to rest. Be truly disconnected to this world's woes and works and be connected fully to the Kingdom of G-d.

Second, "carry this not to the gate" prohibits what had become a regular ungodly occurrence. People were in the habit of coming to Jerusalem on Shabbat to attend the Temple service, and while traveling carrying produce from their fields to sell amid the travel. In Jerusalem, the people sold items at the gate to the villagers and those coming from other towns. This manual labor was forbidden on Sabbath as was buying and selling -- but they had justified it because it was at the gate or at the temple. A reference to this is made in Nehemiah. "Nor bring it in by the gates of Jerusalem": To be unloaded and sold there, as wine, grapes, figs, and fish were..." Nehemiah 13:15.

Contextually speaking, this restriction of carrying a burden was not to be meant as a restriction of carrying a physical item in your hand but rather a restriction of work, buying and selling and carrying the weights of your normal everyday life on Shabbat. The people of Jeremiah's time were breaking Shabbat because they did not honor the meaning of the word "rest".

How did Yeshua deal with this question?

In John 5 we read the story of Yeshua healing a man on Shabbat who had been ill for thirty-eight years. When Yeshua heals him, he tells him to "pick up your mat and walk." In verse 10, the Judean leaders say "It's Shabbat! It's not permitted for you to carry your mat."

Later in the same chapter the leaders begin to persecute Yeshua.

John 5:16-18

Because Yeshua was doing these things on Shabbat, the Judean leaders started persecuting Him. But Yeshua said to them, "My Father is still working, and I also am working." So for this reason the Judean leaders kept trying even harder to kill Him— because He was not only breaking Shabbat, but also calling G-d His own Father, making Himself equal with G-d.

Yeshua makes a fascinating claim here that one might label a contradiction of Torah without digging deeper than the general English translation. He says that His father is still "working" and so He is still "working." Clearly, if we are not supposed to "work" on the Shabbat then this statement only has three possible outcomes. First, Yeshua has been recorded wrong and this is not what he said. This would create many problems and call into question all statements in the gospels. This is not a good option.

Second, He said this and is contradicting the Torah. He is giving a new definition and telling the people that work is okay on Shabbat because our Father in heaven is working on Shabbat. This contradicts Malachi 3:6 in which G-d states, "I the L-rd do not change." G-d is unchanging and that brings us great security. The moment we believe that Messiah has decided to change the law of Shabbat and furthermore tell us that the Father himself is now doing it different is the moment we all throw our hands up in the air and exclaim, "we don't know what to believe." This is not a good option.

Third, Yeshua is stating the truth and we have misunderstood it. This option makes the most sense. Yeshua is perfect and provides for us the perfect law and therefore this writing about Shabbat will reflect that perfection.

Looking deeper into the word translated in English as "work" in this passage, helps us determine what Yeshua meant.

The word used in Greek is ἐργάζομαι *ergazomai.* Vines expository dictionary of the New Testament says the following about this word: Minister (Noun and Verb): "to work, work out, perform," is translated "minister" in 1 Corinthians 9:13. The verb is frequently used of business, or employment, and here the phrase means "those employed in sacred things" or "those who are assiduous in priestly functions."

This word is a noun and verb. As a verb it can mean business work (just as we presume). But it also means "minister." In 1 Corinthians it means to be employed in sacred things or doing of priestly functions. I would argue that in this statement in John, Yeshua was saying the same thing. We know that Yeshua and the

Torah agree that to do "good" for someone on Shabbat is not considered work. To bless, to heal, to feed, to minister is not considered work on Shabbat. When Yeshua says that His father is "still working" we could translate that as His father is "still ministering" or doing good and so Yeshua is still ministering or doing good. Thus, Yeshua is not advocating "work" on Shabbat but rather love expressed through good deeds.

The second area about which the Pharisees wanted to persecute Yeshua comes from a regulation that was also extrapolated from Jeremiah. They had determined that picking up one's mat and walking was the same as "carrying a burden." Many Jews today will not carry anything to synagogue for fear of breaking this command.[1]

But Yeshua tells them that He is only doing what He sees His Father in heaven doing. This means that G-d himself does not consider carrying something or healing someone as a work or burden.

Yeshua defines healing as a blessing and perfectly within the bounds of obedience in Shabbat and He defines carrying one's personal items as acceptable and not a burden in the least.

Yeshua was accused of breaking the Shabbat and was accused of blasphemy as he claimed to be G-d in the flesh. Both accusations, if true, would have prevented him from being the promised Jewish Messiah. However, we see how Yeshua defended against two accusations. First, He clearly explains that the Pharisaical rules (Halachic rules applied today) about work and burden on Shabbat are wrong. Biblical work is defined a vocational broadly and can personally be defined as that which contradicts rest.

After Yeshua defines Shabbat in the proper way, He deals with the claim that He is G-d. Here is His defense:

John 5:37-44

And the Father who sent Me has testified concerning Me. You have never heard His voice nor seen His form. Nor do you have His Word living in you, because you do not trust the One He sent. You search the Scriptures because you suppose that in them you have eternal life. It is these that testify about Me. Yet you are unwilling to come to Me so that you may have life. I do not accept glory from men. But I know you, that you do not have the love of G-d in yourselves. I have come in My Father's name, and you do not receive Me. But if another comes in his own name, you will receive him. How can you believe, when you receive glory from one another, and you do not seek the glory that comes from G-d alone?

Case Closed!

I understand that many of my Jewish friends would accuse me of idol worship because we believe in Yeshua as the Messiah. However, I want to emphasize: Yeshua himself claims that the Father sent Him so that we may have eternal life through having faith in His work of atonement. He will not accept glory from men; He did not come to seek glory. The church many times ascribes glory to Yeshua but I would challenge that as misplaced worship. In truth, we are to worship G-d our Father alone who is in heaven, and we do this through our faith in the Son. We honor the Son of G-d for His great work, and we give love to Him as one who has served. Through Him we have access and boldly and go before the throne of G-d almighty. That is where our worship should be, and Yehovah receives the glory.

Community Protection

Numbers 15:32-36

Once, when the Israelites were in the wilderness, they came upon a man gathering wood on the sabbath day. Those who found him as he was gathering wood brought him before Moses, Aaron, and the whole community. He was placed in custody, for it had not been specified what should be done to him. Then the L-RD said to Moses, "The man shall be put to death: the whole community shall pelt him with stones outside the camp." So, the whole community took him outside the camp and stoned him to death— as the L-RD had commanded Moses.

In the goodness of G-d, we know HE would not require the death of an innocent person or the punishment of a person without reason. Only when that is understood from the complete scriptures can we rightly discern what the above passage means. Simply put, the collector of the wood believed in his way above Yehovah's ways. He seemed determined to be the authority of his own life and therefore was putting the entire community at risk.

In Benson's Commentary is the following explanation of Numbers 15:32:

"A man gathered sticks on the sabbath day–This seems to be mentioned here as an instance of sinning presumptuously; and accordingly, it is so understood by the Jews. The law of the sabbath was plain and positive, and this transgression of it must therefore have been a known and willful sin. And from the connection of this verse with the former it may be justly inferred that this man had sinned with a high hand, despising the word of the L-rd, and the authority of his law." [2]

Many have used this verse to condemn the Jewish people and the law of G-d in the Bible because it seems so outlandish that G-d would order the death of someone for gathering firewood. The sin would not be gathering of wood should it have been required for life. When one reads the Bible and knows the author, G-d, then one can rightly discern the meaning of these verses. The law of G-d is replete with care for the needs of people. The Bible describes the Father as love, servant, benevolent, and good. C.S. Lewis, in writing his famous work,

The Lion the Witch and the Wardrobe, wrote these words about Aslan, (representing G-d in the story) "Safe?" said Mr. Beaver; "don't you hear what Mrs. Beaver tells you? Who said anything about safe? 'Course he isn't safe. But he's good. He's the King, I tell you.'"

—C.S. Lewis, *The Lion, the Witch and the Wardrobe*

G-d may be all powerful and even scary, but he is good.

Sin is never in a vacuum.

I watched a movie called "The Hunt for the Red October." In this film, a Russian sub captain desires to defect to the United States. Another Russian sub captain hunts him. The second captain is full of fire and fury and wants to win so badly that he cannot stop and think logically or be reasonable. As he fires torpedoes, he has been outmaneuvered by the defecting captain. His second in charge tells him, You arrogant *Bleep*, you've killed us!" The torpedo the second captain shot takes out his own sub.

We must understand that when we sin, we put others at risk. Sin does not happen in a vacuum. As I write these words, we have been experiencing a pandemic called the Corona Virus or Covid-19. This virus has left us isolated and separate. We should as a people realize that sin, like a virus, is contagious and can destroy lives.

The man gathering sticks on Shabbat reveals a community holding him accountable for his arrogant disregard for the known law of G-d and putting everyone at risk of being punished. What do I mean by *known* law? Moses did not at that time have a law against picking up sticks on the sabbath. The people seemed to have a problem with it but were not sure what to do. If the law was clear on this, then Moses would not have had to go to G-d and ask what to do. G-d explains that this person had to be put to death which meant that picking up sticks was a bigger sin then the act of picking up sticks indicates on the surface. The community responds properly. This community justice is likened to our modern use of capital punishment or life imprisonment for the one guilty of child molestation or murder. I hear your minds racing now, "But Jeff, picking up sticks is not the same as child molestation or murder, how could you possibly compare the two?"

I agree that child molestation is a much uglier and grievous action than picking up wood. The idea of comparing these two outward acts is almost preposterous. However, if we think about this from a different perspective we may find the differences in the acts are not as far apart as imagined. A man is told by G-d and the Israelite community to honor, guard and keep the Shabbat. In his case this included not working by gathering wood, chopping, starting fires, and possibly preparing for the coming week. This level of disobedience shows the heart of the man was to create his own way in direct disobedience to G-d's ways. The Israelites recognized this and took it to Moses. G-d gives a stunning judgement and sentence. Guilty and death.

Our comparison was the child molester. G-d gives direct commands in scripture to love and teach our children. To do no harm to our children. To raise our children in the admonition of the L-rd. To keep our children safe from sexual immorality and help them be pure in body and heart. A child molester certainly denies G-d's laws and rules and hurts a child in his rebellion. Most would agree that swift and final punishment would not be unjust.

What is the difference? In both scenarios, direct commands are given by G-d and broken by the individual. G-d demands justice. Sin leads to death. It is here where we must be beyond grateful for grace. G-d determines to forgive us through His love and His son's sacrifice on the tree. We repent and receive an atonement that is not deserved nor earned. Thanks be to G-d for the law of sin and death is fulfilled and I am forgiven!

This does not however negate the truth of scripture. Sin has consequences for the individual but there are also community effects. This is why the justice was swift.

The Song of Solomon 2:15 gives us guidance, *"Catch the foxes for us—the little foxes that ruin the vineyards for our vineyards are in blossom."*

The important principle here is if we allow little discrepancies, seemingly smaller violations, among us, then we put the whole community in danger. Remember the adage, "one rotten apple can destroy the entire barrel."

We must be vigilant to catch the little foxes before they grow too big and begin to destroy the vine. For example, of the twelve spies who were sent to search out the promise land, ten came back in fear. They discouraged the community from obeying G-d's command. Those ten costs the Israelites forty years in the wilderness and the loss of the generation.

We must never allow the majority to persuade us to disobey the clear word of G-d.

There was a time in the very recent past when our society would have never accepted the idea that a man could identify as a woman. We would have never imagined a man who identifies as a woman being allowed to go into the same bathroom as little girls. Today we are passing laws to that effect because we have allowed the small foxes to destroy the vine.

We must never allow ourselves to be so prideful as to think we have the right to define sin and punishment. Our task is obedience to the Creator who defines "sin" and "punishment" rather to become our own gods. Many have wandered down this path of self-reliance and self-sustenance without regard for the higher laws of G-d; they have found themselves in destruction and leading others to destruction. Simply put, "pride goes before destruction and a haughty spirit before the fall."[3] Internal actions and thoughts lead to the external behaviors. The Israelites in dealing with the man and his gathering of wood were stopping the problem before the virus spread. For the record, this passage is not a command that anyone who picks up a stick or does something of that nature on Shabbat is required to be executed. This was a recording of a historical moment which gives us insight into the greater principle of obedience to G-d's word. In addition, we must state emphatically that although the *mitzvot* (commands) of G-d are sacred, their interpretations and punishments are not. G-d adjusted His punishments and administered grace many times in the scripture. We should always search for the grace of G-d when we sin and fall short of His glory and His ways.

Shabbat is a great way to reflect upon community health and return to the authority of the scriptures. One of the reasons that Shabbat can be so helpful in keeping a spiritual community healthy is found in the command to keep the Shabbat.

In **Leviticus 23** we read:

Then Adonai spoke to Moses saying: "Speak to Bnei-Yisrael and tell them: These are the appointed moadim of Adonai, which you are to proclaim to be holy convocations—My moadim. Work may be done for six days, but the seventh day is a Shabbat of solemn rest, a holy convocation. You are to do no work—it is a Shabbat to Adonai in all your dwellings.

G-d states through Moses that the appointed times of the L-rd are to be followed and the first one He lists is Shabbat. This is G-d's appointed time. In verse 2, we find another Shabbat nugget related to the community health G-d desires. Shabbat is a time for holy *convocations*.

The Hebrew word for convocation is מִקְרָא (*miqra'*). According to Strong's concordance this word means "something called out, i.e., a public meeting (the act, the persons, or the place); also, a rehearsal, assembly, calling, convocation, reading."

So, on the Shabbat we are called together in assembly. We gather with one another for the purpose of a rehearsal or reading. This is the pattern we also see from the New Testament. As seen in earlier passages in this book, Yeshua went to the synagogue on the Shabbat. Paul attended the synagogue on Shabbat.

The church has been meeting together on Sunday since the late third and early fourth century. The Jewish people have been meeting together on Saturday for at least 3500 years. The Bible states that we should call a time of gathering to read and rehearse the ways of G-d. However, in the New Testament, each time we see a verse that says one of the apostles went into the synagogue on Shabbat it adds the phrase "as was his custom." For example:

Luke 4:16

And he (Yeshua) came to Nazareth, where he had been brought up. And as was his custom, he went to the synagogue on the Sabbath day, and he stood up to read.

Acts 17:1-2

After passing through Amphipolis and Apollonia, they came to Thessalonica, where there was a Jewish synagogue. As was his custom, Paul went to the Jewish people; and for three Shabbatot, he debated the Scriptures with them.

The reason the scripture notes "custom" is because there is not a command on how to gather or assemble. The custom became that the people gathered in synagogues on Shabbat and read the scriptures. This had long been the practice and thus Yeshua continued this practice during his earthly life. The disciples also continued this practice. But this is not the only practice associated with Shabbat.

Acts 2:46-47

And day by day, attending the temple together and breaking bread in their homes, they received their food with glad and generous hearts, praising G-d and having favor with all the people. And the L-rd added to their number day by day those who were being saved.

They met in the Temple courtyard which was a town center. They met in homes, and they ate together. They prayed and sang and witnessed. They did life together. Gathering on Shabbat was the command, but the way of gathering could vary. It is this very act of gathering according to the command of G-d on the seventh day that provides health to a community.

We gather, for example, in our home with people each Friday night Shabbat to have a meal, pray and Bible study. We enjoy the presence of G-d and the joy of fellowship. We are discipling and being discipled. We are gathering on Shabbat.

From time to time, we have larger Shabbat meetings on Saturdays. These gatherings, too, are wonderful and joyous. The point is that we are to use Shabbat as a time of gathering and hearing the word of G-d. How we do that is left to the creative and practical ways people want to gather, being mindful that the pattern of the scripture was in local buildings or in homes.

When all the weekly distractions are removed, we can see more clearly the little foxes in our own lives and in the lives of those with whom we have relationship.

One person we interviewed said this: "Shabbat has been one of the most enlightening things I have had the pleasure of doing. Not only am I fulfilling G-d's word, but I am also able to take time to rest and unload the stresses of the week. Shabbat it like a safe zone G-d gives me once a week to just be protected in a bubble from all outside stresses. When I don't observe Shabbat, my spirit is always off the following week. I have found that in observing I have a deep level of peace and safety that I haven't found anywhere else. I would recommend Shabbat to all people. It's also a great time to get close with your family and laugh with the ones you love."

Supernatural Provision

Exodus 16:29-30

Mark that the L-RD has given you the sabbath; therefore, He gives you two days' food on the sixth day. Let everyone remain where he is: let no one leave his place on the seventh day.

The people remained inactive on the seventh day. For many this would mean sure disaster in their financial world. Here is a testimony from John and Terri.

"In 1977, two young Gentile believers (John and Terri) married and set out to do life together. I had a good job, and we soon bought a new house. She wanted kids so a year or so later we had a first-born son named Joshua. She became a stay-at-home mom. Three years later Nathan came along. Life seemed good but due to increasing inflation and stagnating wages we began to use credit cards and loan refinancing to make ends meet and maintain our lifestyle. Rachel came along in 1987 and things got worse. We were committed believers and immersed in church life. About that time, I discovered Hebrew roots and we even began to tithe for real. The Father blessed and we made ends meet but the debt remained. I started to work overtime on Saturdays trying to pay down the debt, but my family suffered. The Holy Spirit spoke to me about guarding Shabbat and an argument ensued. I saw no way to stay afloat, and I didn't want to lose everything, but I lost the argument. I trusted and stopped working on Shabbat. I then got a promotion and consistent pay increases over the next several years. My wife started a daycare for babies, and we began to diligently pay off our debt. After seven years we had paid off almost a hundred thousand dollars in credit debt without working on Shabbat. Guarding Shabbat gave us Shalom, or rather, made us whole. Praise Yeshua."

One of the challenges for resting on Shabbat is trusting the L-rd and His provision. This was a lesson for the Israelites as they were told that Friday's food provision would last for two days. As time moved forward and they could work for themselves in the land G-d had given them, they had to decide to trust the L-rd regarding the seventh day rest.

Each of us also must decide whether we believe that G-d is our provider. If we choose to accept that Biblical truth, then we can also trust He will sustain us if we do not work on His Shabbat.

Healing on Shabbat

When Yeshua arrived in the first century he was continually challenged by the Pharisees for healing on Shabbat. They had determined that healing on Shabbat was unlawful. However, there is no Biblical precedent for this man-made ruling. Let's learn from Yeshua how he responded.

We read seven times in the Apostolic Writings of the New Testament where Yeshua performed miracles on Shabbat.

1. Cast an unclean spirit out of a man: Mk 1:21-28, Lk 4:31-37

2. Healed Peter's mother-in-law, who had a fever: Mt 8:14-15, Mk 1:29-31, Lk 4:38-39

3. Healed the man with the withered hand: Mt 12:9-13, Mk 3:1-6, Lk 6:6-11

4. Healed the lame man by the pool of Bethesda: Jn 5:1-18

5. Healed the crippled woman: Lk 13:10-17

6. Healed the man with dropsy: Lk 14:1-6

7. Healed the man born blind: Jn 9:1-7,14

Let's take a look at a couple of these.

Luke 14:1-6

Now when Yeshua went into the home of one of the leaders of the Pharisees to eat a meal on Shabbat, they were watching Him closely. And there before Him was a man swollen with fluid. So Yeshua said to the Torah lawyers and the Pharisees, "Is it permitted to heal on Shabbat, or not?"

But they kept silent. So Yeshua took hold of him and healed him, and He sent him away. Then He said to them, "Which of you, with a son or an ox falling into a well on Yom Shabbat, will not immediately pull him out?" And they could not reply to these things."

A few observations: Yeshua ate a meal with the Pharisees on Shabbat. He did not isolate himself to his followers alone. He engaged with non-followers around the dinner table.

His asked them a question rather arguing. He knew what they believed and gave them an opportunity to share their views on healing on Shabbat. Yeshua then gave them a life example of how it is permitted, even by their standards, to help in a life-threatening situation.

Yeshua endorsed healing and acts of kindness on Shabbat. This was a perfect opportunity to validate Pharisaical authority, but He stood on Biblical authority.

Yeshua confirms this again in another Shabbat encounter in:

Luke 13:10-17

Now Yeshua was teaching in one of the synagogues on Shabbat. And behold, there was a woman with a disabling spirit for eighteen years, bent over and completely unable to stand up straight. When Yeshua saw her, He called out to her and said, "Woman, you are set free from your disability." Then He laid hands on her, and instantly she stood up straight and began praising G-d.

But the synagogue leader, indignant that Yeshua had healed on Shabbat, started telling the crowd, "There are six days in which work should be don't—so come to be healed on those days and not on Yom Shabbat!"

But the L-rd answered him and said, "Hypocrites! On Shabbat doesn't each of you untie his ox or donkey from the stall and lead it away to give it drink? So this one, a daughter of Abraham incapacitated by Satan for eighteen years, shouldn't she be set free from this imprisonment on Yom Shabbat?" When Yeshua said these things, all His opponents were put to shame; but the whole crowd was rejoicing at all the glorious things done by Him.

The Pharisees clung to their man-made rule that you can be healed on any day except Shabbat. Yeshua once again answered: How is it permissible to take care of your ox or donkey but not untether someone held in bondage to the works of Satan? He refutes their man-made interpretations of work and confirms that healing is not work.

Yeshua gives us the balance of forbidden work and permissible good deeds. Those who work as doctors, firefighters or police officers, or any array of first responders are not profaning Shabbat by discharging their duties to help others. The focus on Shabbat is not centered around being afraid that you may make a mistake and "work" but rather that your heart desires to put aside work for a day. Your heart wants to put off the things you do the other six days of the week and truly enter into a renewal of the covenant through rest.

This is a critical understanding of work verses rest. G-d always allowed good works, kindness on Shabbat, as well as helping responses to emergencies. There is no fear of breaking the Shabbat when helping someone, healing someone, or caring for a person in need--including yourself.

This is Shabbat. Rest is not just the absence of work but is the inclusion of the presence and power of connecting to G-d and others.

My study of scripture leads me to conclude that work comes in many forms, and you must hear G-d to determine if the activities you are doing on the Shabbat are true work. G-d is faithful. If you seek Him, He will tell you what is lawful. His desire is for you to enter the sacred rest of His presence. We cannot limit G-d to our man-made definitions of work.

You will most certainly be able to tell if you are resting. As each Shabbat approaches you will find yourself craving that time set aside to rest. As you do this you will know the gift of Shabbat has come upon you.

Jeff Friedlander

THE SACRED SPACE:
WHAT MAKES SPACE HOLY?

I come downstairs from my office at our home to the weekly aroma of Friday afternoon challah bread coming out of the oven. It fills my senses and signals that Shabbat is only hours away. My wife has been working most of the day, cleaning and cooking to prepare our home to greet our Shabbat dinner guests as we all welcome in the Shabbat. In addition to physical preparations, my wife, Sherri, is preparing the spiritual atmosphere through song and prayer. She sets the table for our dinner and prays over each chair and table setting. She creates a beautiful spirit within the house so that everyone who comes will sense that G-d is doing something special. She knows this night is not like all other nights for this night is the beginning of Shabbat.

With the preparations made, our guests arrive and we welcome them into our home as family. They have become more than just visitors.

We stand around the kitchen, talk about the week and check how everyone is feeling. We then sit down to a specially set table and Sherri prepares to light the Shabbat candles.

The lighting of the candles is a beautiful tradition we embrace to set apart the Shabbat from the rest of the week. It is not a Biblical command for Shabbat but rather a way to mark this special time. Sherri invites us all to pause and prepare our hearts to enter this holy appointment with Adonai. As the candles are lit and she says a blessing, the light reaches for the ceiling and touches each of us in a different way. We say a robust, "Shabbat Shalom" as we enter our appointed time of rest for the week.

We all begin to reflect on our blessings as we just marked the beginning of Shabbat. The scripture says that G-d marked the seasons and days with the sun and the moon and tonight we marked the Shabbat with the light of a candle.

Sherri explains that not only do these candles represent the time of Shabbat has begun but they are beautiful reminders that we are to be the light of the world. We were given a directive by Messiah Yeshua to go and be the light of the world. Light dispels darkness. No matter how dark a room may be when a candle is lit the darkness is expelled.

The Bible says that as a follower of Yeshua the Messiah, you are the temple of the Holy Spirit, the dwelling place of G-d. You house His glorious presence and therefore the light that shines are not of your own doing but is G-d illuminating through you.

When the first Temple was built in Jerusalem by Solomon, son of King David, the Holy of Holies filled the very back of the structure. It housed the holy Ark of the Covenant and only the High Priest could enter the holy of holies, and only once a year. The Ark contained the staff that Aaron used in Egypt to confront Pharoah. This special staff budded as a sign of Aaron's and Moshes' anointing from G-d. This staff represented G-d's authority and communicated the idea that under Him we have been given authority over darkness and rebellion.

In addition to the staff, the Ark housed the tablets upon which G-d had written His ten commandments. These words represent the categories upon which all the law was written. G-d's law, by design, teaches us how to walk out our salvation daily. The law or instruction shows us the proper way to treat one another, the way to approach G-d and the way to grow spiritually. The law was never a means to salvation but rather a means to holy living after salvation. This law was preserved in the form of the ten commandments or in Hebrew statements. The fourth statement refers to the Shabbat.

The law was never a means to salvation

but rather a means to holy living after salvation

Exodus 20:8-11

Remember the Sabbath day, to keep it holy. Six days you shall labor, and do all your work, but the seventh day is a Sabbath to the L-rd your G-d. On it you shall not do any work, you, or your son, or your daughter, your male servant, or your female servant, or your livestock, or the sojourner who is within your gates. For in six days the L-rd made heaven and earth, the sea, and all that is in them, and rested on the seventh day. Therefore the L-rd blessed the Sabbath day and made it holy.

This great commandment lives in the Ark of the Covenant.

The Homes of G-d

Over the course of human history, G-d has chosen four physical places to call His home on the earth.

First, the garden of Eden. He created it in six days, put life in it and then walked among that life and had relationship with that life. The garden was the first house of G-d and the first sacred place.

Second, the Tabernacle and later the Temple. In these places G-d said He would put His presence and dwell with man.

Third, the city of Jerusalem. G-d said he had chosen a place on the earth to dwell, and that place was Jerusalem where He would put His name. In ancient Hebraic understanding, the name represented the person completely. When G-d put His name on Jerusalem, G-d Himself was home there.

Lastly, we are told that when we are born-again, we are filled with the *Ruach Hakodesh* (the Holy Spirit), and we become the temple (house) of G-d.

All these places have something in common: They are sacred because they house G-d and His law. In each of G-d's dwelling places He coexists with His law or commands.

In the garden, He commanded the created human not to eat from one particular tree. Grave consequences flowed from breaking that command. When the tabernacle and later temple were built, G-d placed his law physically in the structures and gave them to the people through his servants and by His spirit. When His commands were violated, there were again grave consequences. When G-d put His name in Jerusalem, the people of Israel were given commands to follow; when those commands were broken, grave consequences ensued. Finally, as we are born again and G-d places his Spirit in us, it comes with His laws, commands, statutes and when they are broken we suffer grave consequences.

Yeshua commented on this in **Matthew 5:17-20:**

Do not think that I have come to abolish the Law or the Prophets; I have not come to abolish them but to fulfill them. For truly, I say to you, until heaven and earth pass away, not an iota, not a dot, will pass from the Law until all is accomplished. Therefore, whoever relaxes one of the least of these commandments and teaches others to do the same will be called least in the kingdom of heaven, but whoever does them and teaches them will be called great in the kingdom of heaven. For I tell you, unless your righteousness exceeds that of the scribes and Pharisees, you will never enter the kingdom of heaven.

Without question, His followers are to read, teach and follow the law and the prophets until heaven and earth disappear. If we relax even what is considered the least of the commandments, then we are least in the kingdom.

G-d expects us to keep His commands. However, for many this is difficult to consider because our traditions have taught us that most of the "laws or commands" in the Old Testament no longer apply. However, Yeshua spoke to all who claim to be part of His kingdom. How we became a part of his kingdom is foundational to being able to keep Shabbat.

Yeshua knew that being born again, being a son of the King, and servant of the Kingdom did not happen because of obedience to the law and the prophets. Becoming a child of G-d only happens through grace from G-d and our faith. When we repent and turn to G-d we are saved. Some may argue and say, "Wait a minute, Jeff, repentance is work and therefore, you are wrong." The foundation of the ministry of Yeshua (Jesus) was repentance.

Matthew 4:13-17

And leaving Nazareth he went and lived in Capernaum by the sea, in the territory of Zebulun and Naphtali, so that what was spoken by the prophet Isaiah might be fulfilled:

"The land of Zebulun and the land of Naphtali,

the way of the sea, beyond the Jordan, Galilee of the Gentiles—

the people dwelling in darkness

have seen a great light,

and for those dwelling in the region and shadow of death,

on them a light has dawned."

From that time Jesus began to preach, saying, "Repent, for the kingdom of heaven is at hand."

Repentance was a key ingredient to relationship. Peter, one of the very first to be called to Yeshua and to be trained at His side, understood the way of salvation better than anyone. After he and 119 others were baptized in the Holy Spirit on Shavuot (Pentecost) in a room in Jerusalem, Peter went into the temple courtyard and gave a testimony. He explained the history of the Jewish people and how G-d had sent Yeshua to be their Messiah. The account continued:

Acts 2:37-41

Now when they heard this, they were cut to the heart and said to Peter and the rest of the emissaries, "Fellow brethren, what shall we do?"

Peter said to them, "Repent, and let each of you be immersed in the name of Messiah Yeshua for the removal of your sins, and you will receive the gift of the Ruach ha-Kodesh. For the promise is for you and your children, and for all who are far away—as many as Adonai our G-d calls to Himself."

With many other words he warned them and kept urging them, saying, 'Save yourselves from this twisted generation!' So those who received his message were immersed, and that day about three thousand souls were added.

Notice that repentance came first when those convicted by the Holy Spirit of their lawbreaking sin sought guidance. Turn from sin; turn back to G-d. Be immersed in the name of G-d through Yeshua's sacrifice. Then receive forgiveness and the Holy Spirit.

I must assume that Peter understood the salvation process better than the theologians that would follow. I must assume that repentance under G-d's definition does not constitute a work on my part. Rather it is a response to the conviction of the Holy Spirit of G-d as He reaches out to me and convicts me of my sin. By faith, I respond with repentance and in a confession of faith in Messiah Yeshua as the sacrificed son of G-d, atonement dawns. As such, I am born again by "faith, not works that any man should boast."

Once we have repented and accepted by faith the atoning work of Messiah Yeshua we become a sacred place where G-d dwells. In the Ark, the law of G-d is housed, marking that where G-d dwells is holy and sacred. His law is sacred. Where He places His name, He places His law: That synthesis becomes The Sacred. That synthesis also unfolds within us.

He writes the law of G-d upon our hearts. When we transgress that law, we must repent. The tablets of G-d's law were physically in the Ark but through Yeshua they are now in us. As the temple of the Holy Spirit, we have the responsibility to safeguard and keep the laws of G-d. As a sacred place we are expected to guard and keep the fourth commandment; ignoring the commands that were placed in the Ark and now dwelling in our hearts brings grave consequences.

Physical Sacred Space

The Bible does not say where to have this holy convocation. The Bible simply instructs us to gather. Two common ways to gather and honor Shabbat are the synagogue and the home.

In our modern world, the most common sacred space is in a building that houses more people than possible in a home. Synagogues use buildings as a sacred space to gather for a holy convocation, gathering on Shabbat to worship the G-d of Abraham, Isaac, and Jacob. This gathering on Shabbat sanctifies these physical places. They become set apart for a holy purpose and G-d joins join with those that are honoring His word.

As you enter your building of worship ask yourself a question. Do I feel something different here than other buildings I go into? A holy and sacred space can touch a person. Our buildings should house more than just the people of G-d, they should house the holiness and glory of G-d just as the tabernacle did.

But what about our physical home? Is that a sacred place?

Years ago, we began to see a great message evolve that essentially said the church was not a building but rather the people of G-d. This is so true. When the first and even second century followers of Messiah met together, they were normally under some persecution. They met in homes and many times in secret but even under those restrictions, they carried power and influence. The growth of the body of Messiah could not be denied as it literally overtook the known world. Faith in Yeshua as L-rd became the prevailing religion of the ancient world, notably and predominantly without major buildings or structures.

However, that does not negate G-d's anointing on a physical place as sacred, holy, and special. All throughout the scripture, G-d puts a special mark on buildings, lands, cities, and homes. As far back as Abraham's grandson, Jacob, anointing of a place was common.

Genesis 28:18

"So early in the morning Jacob took the stone that he had put under his head and set it up for a pillar and poured oil on the top of it...."

Additionally, we read multiple places about G-d's anointing of the Tabernacle and the Temple. In fact, there was a command to sacrifice, and to use blood, wine, and oil to anoint the Temple building and the furniture within.

In **Matthew 10:11-13**

And whatever town or village you enter, find out who is worthy in it and stay there until you depart. As you enter the house, greet it. And if the house is worthy, let your peace come upon it, but if it is not worthy, let your peace return to you.

Here Yeshua states that as the disciples go to a home to stay while sharing the gospel in that town, they carry an anointing to put on that host home. They can give it peace--or take peace away.

This peace affected the residents. I have entered homes that are saturated with the peace of G-d, and I could feel His presence upon entering. Conversely, I have entered homes that are full of the world and do not have the presence of G-d and could feel the anxiety and lack of peace.

Simply put, the body of Messiah is people, not buildings or homes. Nonetheless, anointing can rest on buildings and homes. Others can sense the power and presence of the L-rd the minute they enter a structure. Yes, your home and mine are to be sacred places.

We are the temple of the Holy Spirit, but our homes are to be an extension of the presence of G-d in our lives. In Hebraic thought, it is not one or the other but "Yes and Amen." Both the home and the body can be a temple to house G-d's presence on the earth.

So many times, we think of our home as *our* sanctuary rather than G-d's. We view our home as our space that we can treat as we wish rather than a sacred place G-d wants to dwell and bring His shalom. Let us all begin to hold the home as a sacred space of G-d's dwelling!

Holy Convocation

On Shabbat we gather in our homes in obedience to the law of G-d which is stored in the Ark and simultaneously resides in us. In Leviticus 23, we are told to call a holy convocation, meaning a set apart gathering. These words describe a gathering of people, whether your immediate family, your friends or a full congregation or fellowship. We gather on Shabbat to set the day apart and keep it holy, to encourage one another in the faith, to study the word of G-d together, and learn from one another. We worship together and declare the wonders of our G-d. This holy convocation refocuses our attention onto G-d, encourages our faith and prepares us to be the light to the nations during the week.

Matthew 18:20

Where two or more are gathered in my name, I am there in their midst.

Our homes are the places that G-d has given us to dwell and are the first places we must rule. The rulership of the home is the ground that builds the city which builds the nation which builds the kingdom.

A Lesson from the Movies

179

Our family loves movies. We have two favorite movies we watch at specific times of the year. We watch our absolute favorite of all time, *Fiddler on the Roof,* during Passover. This is a story revolving around a Ukrainian Jewish community facing a pogrom. We enjoy the music, the comedy, and the interplay of the characters. Most of all we love to see the truth of scripture being played out on a big screen. A traditional approach to Judaism is tested and goes through cultural pressure to change. Without the Bible as the standard the traditions adjust, and with that the family goes through dramatic and stressful shifts. The home life changes. The home itself gets a reboot in its structure and that comes from the changing culture outside. The story is great, but the reality is somewhat difficult to see. As the movie gives us a glimpse, we watch two great stories at the same time. One is the changing dynamic of a family being forced to choose traditions or culture as its practice. The Tanakh seems to be missing but not a love of G-d or a desire to have G-d in the midst. The second story is the larger attack on the community itself. This timeframe is when the Soviet Union issues decrees and removes Jews from their homes by force, leaving them nowhere to go. Already impoverished, they must now try to survive finding a new home. This is the bigger picture and the one that is so painful to see.

Yet both stories are one. The home is the center of the community, and the smaller story of changing traditions is no different than the larger story of stronger community imposing its will on small community. Both stories simply are the culture deciding for the family how they will live.

Is this G-d's way? Certainly not. In fact, the Bible challenges each of us to realize our responsibility as priest of our own home. Our domain must be a protected space for the King to come and the kingdom to grow.

Our homes face many challenges today. We are all being pressured to live as the culture lives—life that does not honor or even know G-d.

The following story by an unknown author helps us understand:

The Stranger

A few months before I was born, my dad met a stranger who was new to our small Tennessee town. From the beginning, Dad was fascinated with this enchanting newcomer, and soon invited him to live with our family. The stranger was quickly accepted and was around to welcome me into the world a few months later. As I grew up, I never questioned his place in our family. Mom taught me to love the Word of G-d. Dad taught me to obey it. But the stranger was our storyteller. He could weave the most fascinating tales. Adventures, mysteries, and comedies were daily conversations. He could hold our whole family spellbound for hours each evening. He was like a friend to the whole family. He took Dad, Bill, and me to our first major league baseball game. He was always encouraging us to see the movies and he even made arrangements to introduce us to several movie stars. The stranger was an incessant talker. Dad didn't seem to mind, but sometimes Mom would quietly get up - while the rest of us were enthralled with one of his stories of faraway places - and go to her room to read her Bible and pray. I wonder now if she ever prayed that the stranger would leave. You see, my dad ruled our household with certain moral convictions. But this stranger never felt an obligation to honor them. Profanity, for example, was not allowed in our house - not from us, from our friends, or adults. Our longtime visitor, however, used occasional four-letter words that burned my ears and made Dad squirm. To my knowledge the stranger was never confronted. My dad was a teetotaler who didn't permit alcohol in his home - not even for cooking. But the stranger felt he needed exposure and enlightened us to other ways of life. He offered us beer and other alcoholic beverages often. He made cigarettes look tasty, cigars manly, and pipes distinguished. He talked freely (too much too freely) about sex. His comments were sometimes blatant, sometimes suggestive, and generally embarrassing. I know now that my early concepts of the man/woman relationship were influenced by the stranger. As I look back, I believe it was the grace of G-d that the stranger did not influence us more. Time after time he opposed the values of my parents. Yet he was seldom rebuked and never asked to leave. More than thirty years have passed since the stranger moved in with the young family on Morningside Drive. But if I were to walk into my parents' den today, you would still see him sitting over in a corner, waiting for someone to listen to him talk and watch him draw his pictures. His name? We always called him TV.

Yes, today the electronic/media influence is so great that children as young as two and three are already playing with their phones and learning to live through them. Culture pressed in, and who do you think gives culture its marching orders? When G-d is not in a space, the enemy fills the void. The Satan is evil and has many followers both in the unseen realm and the natural realm who will do the work of influence the way he wants it done. Technology is his great mouthpiece.

We must realize our home is a sacred space and it must be protected with a vengeance. Yeshua in his great sermon on the mount stated in

Matthew 11:12 (ESV):

From the days of John the Baptist until now the kingdom of heaven has suffered violence, and the violent take it by force.

This kingdom warrants our fight. This kingdom is at war, and we are its the frontline warriors. Our number one battle ground is our home. It is the sacred space G-d must have dominion over. The kingdom cannot happen in the city, the state, or the nation, if it does not happen in the home.

My family's second favorite movie on the annual viewing list is *It's a Wonderful Life*. The lead character, George Bailey, is caught up in a battle to leave the town in which he was raised. He fights his entire life to get out, until he is shown the real blessing of being there. In one scene, he tells the malicious Mr. Potter what he thinks of him and what he thinks of his own father.

Just a minute... just a minute. Now, hold on, Mr. Potter. You're right when you say my father was no businessman. I know that. Why he ever started this cheap, penny-ante Building and Loan, I'll never know. But neither you nor anyone else can say anything against his character, because his whole life was... why, in the 25 years since he and his brother, Uncle Billy, started this thing, he never once thought of himself. Isn't that right, Uncle Billy? He didn't save enough money to send Harry away to college, let alone me. But he did help a few people get out of your slums, Mr. Potter, and what's wrong with that? Why... here, you're all businessmen here. Doesn't it make them better citizens? Doesn't it make them better customers? You... you said... what'd you say a minute ago? They had to wait and save their money before they even ought to think of a decent home. Wait? Wait for what? Until their children grow up and leave them? Until they're so old and broken down that they... Do you know how long it takes a working man to save $5,000? Just remember this, Mr. Potter, that this rabble you're talking about... they do most of the working and paying and living and dying in this community. Well, is it too much to have them work and pay and live and die in a couple of decent rooms and *a bath? Anyway, my father didn't think so. People were human beings to him. But to you, a warped, frustrated old man, they're cattle. Well in my book, my father died a much richer man than you'll ever be!*

Yes, the much richer man understood that helping people have a home of their own meant something vital. In fact, when he gave the keys to one of the other characters in the movie, they toasted the new home:

"BREAD that this house may never know hunger, SALT that life may always have flavor and WINE that joy and prosperity may reign forever."

What a feeling. Your home is to be treasured. It does not matter if you rent, own, or live in an apartment, townhome, or mansion. The point is: Your domain is protected, prepared, and honored as the sanctuary of the Living G-d.

I pray that as you go forward and gather in a holy convocation at your building or home you will begin to pray in such power that G-d Himself will make the physical structure a true sanctuary for His presence!

THE SACRED TRUTH:
BUY THE TRUTH AND SELL IT NOT

"There is no absolute truth. There is only your truth." **Debasish Mridha**

This ideology has recked many a soul. It encapsulates the concept of 'relativism.'

> "Relativism reduces every element of absoluteness to relativity while making a completely illogical exception in favor of this reduction itself... one might just as well say that there is no language or write that there is no writing. The assertion nullifies itself if it is true and by nullifying itself logically proves thereby that it is false; its initial absurdity lies in the implicit claim to be unique in escaping, as if by enchantment, from a relativity that is declared to be the only possibility."[1]

Obviously, absolutes do exist, and truth is an absolute. My perspective, interpretation and application of a truth may be different than another person's but that does not negate nor change the actual truth. Truth stands alone. This should be liberating rather than restrictive.

To me, truth is grand. Truth expands my mind and allows my imagination to grow. Truth provides a grounding that allows exploration without becoming lost. In navigation terms, truth is true north. True north is a fixed point in a spinning world. It is a way of direction for us to focus and get our bearings. For us to live life in the manner that G-d desires we must find true north in every issue and context.

True North is the path that G-d directs us to even though He has allowances to go from east to west on the way to north. Truth then becomes the compass and the boundary line that keep a person from falling into confusion and discouragement.

Bumper Theology

When we took our kids bowling, they would raise up bumpers in the gutters so that the kids' balls would make it all the way down the lane to the pins. As small children, their balls would roll from one side of the lane to the other as it would hit the bumper and continue its journey to the goal. In life with G-d, He has bumpers set up for us to crisscross the lane of life on the way to true north. The goal is to hit the targets that He has already preplanned and set. That's "bumper theology."

Even as you begin to learn about Shabbat and seek the L-rd in understanding it practically, I pray that you will find His truth.

In this book, I have shared many things from the Bible about Shabbat. However, people have debated the truth of things shared here for thousands of years. How can truth then have so many faces and which face is truth?

Many people give up on the search for G-d and His ways. We argue over truth so much that we begin to fight for our position instead of His truth. Truth then becomes the victim rather than the victor.

I pray that you let no arguments and debates defeat your desire for G-d's truth and His way. Shabbat is a great blessing of life and a gift for those that desire Him. My encouragement to you is to allow the sacred truth of Shabbat to find its way into your practical and spiritual life. Each time you obey the word of G-d, you will find clarity of instruction and incredible joy.

The truth of Shabbat is that G-d desired for each of us to receive from Him a gift of 24 hours of rest, rejuvenation, connection, and restoration. We are given this great opportunity and yet most have either rejected it or never had it explained to them as a gift for all. I pray for you that this book has opened your heart up to the gift of Shabbat and the blessing of walking in His ways.

Conclusion: What do I do now?

First, pray over what you have read. Search out the scriptures in this book and others that seem to apply and ask G-d to clarify this for you. Allow the *Ruach HaKodesh*, Holy Spirit, to teach you as He promised He would.

Once you have concluded that Shabbat is a gift from G-d and that G-d desires for you to put this ancient practice into your life, then the steps become clear.

Plan each Friday evening to Saturday evening to be a day of rest. The first appendix is a guide to Shabbat practices that can be used to help you in the beginning.

Do only that which glorifies G-d and keeps His command of doing no work and resting and honoring creation. Follow the example of Yeshua in seeking out scriptures and having discussions and prayers with family and friends. Enjoy fellowship with people and be bound only to the principle of no labor as it relates to vocational normal work. Be free to be kind and do good deeds for others as G-d leads. As you enter this time of rest you will begin to catch the spirit of Shabbat rather than the laws of Shabbat. May we all stay in the spirit of this appointed time.

For those of you that have jobs requiring Saturday work, our suggestion is that you pray for a creative way to change your hours. We have heard numerous testimonies of people who desired to have Shabbat and when they prayed and spoke to their employer a way was made for them. G-d will honor your desire as you are honoring His command. It may take a few weeks or even months to adjust your work schedule if you normally work on Shabbat but trust the L-rd and He will make a way. He is a miracle worker.

Because this book is about Shabbat from a scriptural perspective, we have not spent much time on modern practices within those communities that do practice Shabbat. The most well-known community that practices Shabbat would be the Jewish community and the strictest sect of that community would be the Orthodox. We have included in the appendix some of the understanding the Orthodox bring to the keeping of Shabbat. For those of you who are not familiar with their view we have provided an explanation at the beginning of the appendix.

Also, please feel free to write or contact Be One Ministries for questions or to have us at an event.

APPENDICES

Jeff Friedlander

SHABBAT DINNER GUIDE

This is a guide we prepared for people to use in their homes as they begin to observe Shabbat. Please use and distribute as you desire.

Shalom Chevarim (Peace Friends),

We are delighted you have decided to join with us in the celebration of Shabbat. This is a time G-d has set for us to meet with Him. The following is a resource to help you celebrate Shabbat as a weekly part of your faith walk.

We encourage families to practice Shabbat around the dinner table. We also encourage you to expand the borders of your tent (Isaiah 54:2), by inviting friends to join you as you enter the rest of the L-rd. This is a joyous celebration – it's like a holiday every week. We pray that your tables are filled with laughter, connections, inspiration and are refreshing as you connect one to another and to the Father.

Good things happen around the table!

Rabbi Jeff and Sherri Friedlander

Use the following summaries to help explain to people your new practice of Shabbat.

What is Shabbat?

Did you know that G-d has set an appointment with you weekly? This *moed* or appointed time is on His calendar. He calls it Shabbat. This is the first appointment G-d set with us after creation in Genesis 2:1-3. The Scripture teaches that, "He blessed the seventh day and made it holy." Shabbat has been set apart by G-d since creation.

Why did G-d do this?

The Scripture again gives us the answer, "Because on it he rested from all the work of creating that he had done."

G-d instituted a day of rest for his people from their busy work weeks. After G-d brought the chaotic space into order through creation, he created a home to share with his human family. Shabbat is a time to step away from the chaos and distractions of everyday life and enter rest.

Shabbat was confirmed in writing after the exodus of Israel from Egypt (Exodus 20:8-11). By remembering Shabbat, Israel would remember who was the G-d of gods, the Master of creation. They would be reminded that G-d loved them from the beginning. Israel did not have to earn G-d's love, only rest in it.

Yeshua and his disciples also observed Shabbat. Yeshua even taught and healed on Shabbat (Mark 1:21) stirring up controversy with the Pharisees. It was his custom to go to synagogue on Shabbat (Luke 4:16). When speaking about the end of the age, Yeshua says, "Pray that your escape will not happen in the winter or on Shabbat." Yeshua did not come to abolish Shabbat but rather to provide the sacrifice necessary which allows us to enter the presence of the Living G-d and rest.

Shabbat is an appointed time (*moed*) with G-d for all believers to remember that G-d is our master over chaos, our creator, and our deliverer. We can all cease from our weekly work and enter the rest of the L-rd.

When is Shabbat?

"And on the seventh day G-d finished his work that he had done, and he rested on the seventh day. So, G-d blessed the seventh day and made it holy…" Gen 2:1

Genesis 1:5 says, "…there is evening and there is morning, the first day." Therefore, Shabbat begins at sundown of Friday and ends at sundown on Saturday.

What is a Shabbat Dinner?

Today, many believers celebrate Shabbat in a worship service, however, this does not capture the fullness of Shabbat. We've lost the meaning and richness of Shabbat and we must recover this appointed time with G-d.

Shabbat is the Hebrew word that is translated into English as "Sabbath" and means "rest". Some people will say to one another "Shabbat shalom" which means, "Peace on the Shabbat," or more figuratively, "May you dwell in complete wholeness on this seventh day, the day of rest."

Shabbat dinner is not a Biblical mandate but rather a way the Jewish community has honored Shabbat for centuries. Gathering around the dinner table as a family, entering Shabbat to rest from ordinary work and being refreshed as a family for a twenty-four hour period.

Shabbat dinners are a time to draw family together around the kingdom of G-d. Many times, prayers are prayed over the children, scripture is discussed and laughter around the table can be heard as the family reconnects each week.

The world G-d intended for humanity was cursed because of the fall of man (Genesis 3:17-19). Eden was lost. Shabbat is a reminder of what G-d desired – and still desires – for us to be at home with Him and at peace (shalom) with our brothers and sisters. When G-d made a covenant with Israel at Mount Sinai

(Exodus 24:1-8), He invited Moses, Aaron, his sons, and the elders of Israel to a meal with Him on Mount Sinai (Exodus 24:9-10). G-d then gave Moses the tablets of the Law (Exodus 24:12-18). G-d's celebration of having a family was not conditioned on the giving of the Law.

Prophetically, Shabbat dinners give us a look into the future when we will all be at G-d's table with Yeshua as our host, complete in his deliverance from the present world. Shabbat, therefore, is a rehearsal and brief glimpse into the age yet to come.

Practicing Shabbat provides a set aside time for family fellowship with G-d, to worship, remember, reflect, and rest. Shabbat dinners are a joyful and festive meal where we mark the beginning of our twenty-four hour rest.

SHABBAT DINNER ELEMENTS:

(All items can be found at major supermarkets)

- Candle (2)
- Wine or grape juice
- Challah Bread or matzah

POSSIBLE ORDER OF SHABBAT DINNER

1. Prayer of Welcome
2. Lighting the candles
3. Hamotzi (blessing over the bread)
4. Kiddush (blessing over the wine/grape juice)
5. Dinner
6. Parasha group discussion
7. Prayer and blessings over members
8. Shema

Here are some scriptures to reflect on about Shabbat.

Genesis 2:3

So G-d blessed the seventh day and made it holy, because on it G-d rested from all his work that he had done in creation.

Deuteronomy 5:15

You shall remember that you were a slave in the land of Egypt, and the L-rd your Go brought you out from there with a mighty hand and an outstretched arm. Therefore, the L-rd your G-d commanded you to keep the Shabbat day.

Mark 2:27

And he said to them, "The Shabbat was made for man, not man for the Shabbat. Therefore, the Son of Man is L-rd even of the Shabbat."

Hebrews 4:3, 9-10

For we who have believed enter that rest...

So then there remains a Shabbat rest for the people of G-d, for whoever has entered G-d's rest has also rested from his works as G-d did from his.

Isaiah 66:22-12

For as new heavens and the new earth that I make shall remain before me, says the L-rd, so shall your offspring and your name remain. From new moon to new moon, and from Shabbat to Shabbat, all flesh shall come to worship before me, declares the L-rd.

Description of Shabbat Dinner

A Shabbat dinner is more than just a dinner party or small group gathering. Our G-d has set an appointment with us so that we may be empowered by Him and have a rest from our ordinary work. A Shabbat dinner is a great way to begin this *moed* (appointed time). The Jewish community has developed some meaningful traditions that set this day apart from the rest of the week.

The dinner begins with the lighting of the candles at sundown. It is traditionally performed by the woman of the house. This draws our attention to the *menorah* (golden lampstand) in the temple that resided in the Holy Place. The *menorah* is a seven branched light that signified G-d's presence. Yeshua is the light of the world (John 8:12: 9:5). We are also to be the light of the world because we are members of the Body of Messiah (Matthew 5:14). The lights of our Shabbat dinner signal that we are entering into a Holy place and time. The candle lighting marks the separation from the ordinary work week into the glorious rest of the L-rd where we enjoy the light of His presence.

The woman will light the two candles and may gently wave her hands over the flames to bring the light towards her face and/or wave her hands over the flame to push the light towards the guests. She then covers her eyes and recites the messianic blessing.

A head cover is optional.

BLESSINGS FOR THE CANDLES

ברוך אתה יהוה אלהינו מלך העורם

אשר קדשנו בדברן

ונתן לנו את ישוע משיחנו

וצונו להיות אור לעולם

Baruch atah Adonai, Eloheinu Melech ha-olam, asher kid'shanu bidvaro, v'natan lanu et Yeshua M'shicheinu, v'tzivanu l'hiyot or l'olam.

Blessed are You Adonai, our G-d, King of the universe, Who has sanctified us with his Word, and has given us Yeshua our Messiah, and commanded us to be light to the world.

Optional: Saying after the lighting of the candles.

"Come, let us welcome Shabbat,

Light reminds us of G-d; The L-rd is my light and my salvation.

Light reminds us of His image within us; "The human spirit is the light of the L-rd."

Light reminds us of G-d's covenant with us.

"For the mitzvah is a lamp and the Torah is a light."

Light reminds us of Israel's calling.

"I have made you a covenant people, a light to the nations."

Light reminds us of the world to come.

"In that day they will need no light for the L-rd G-d will give them light."

Light reminds us of the Messiah.

He said: "I am the light of the world."

Come, let us welcome Shabbat, and to G-d sing praise, and pray for His eternal Shabbat, the end of days.

HAMOTZI - BLESSING OVER THE BREAD

Bread is a gift from G-d. We are reminded that G-d provided daily *manna* for the Hebrew children while they were in the desert (Exodus 16:4, Psalm 78:24-25) He is our PROVIDER. We are reminded that He is a MULTIPLIER as we remember that he miraculously feed the multitudes. (Matthew 14:13-21). We remember that He is our REDEEMER as he transformed the bread of affliction of the first Passover to the bread of LIFE at the last Passover Yeshua celebrated on the earth. (Commonly known as The Last Supper or Communion) (Matthew 26:26). Finally, we are reminded that "man does not live by bread alone but by every word that proceeds out of the mouth of G-d." (Matt 4:4)

Traditionally the man of the home lifts the Challah (braided bread) and recites the Hamotzi. After reciting the blessing, the bread is then passed around for each guest to take a piece to eat.

BLESSING

בָּרוּךְ אַתָּה יהוה אֱלֹהֵינוּ מֶלֶךְ הָעוֹלָם הַמּוֹצִיא לֶחֶם מִן הָאָרֶץ

Baruch a-tah Adonai E-lo-hey-nu me-lech ha-olam ha-motzi le-chem min ha-or-rets

Blessed are you, L-rd our G-d, King of the universe, who brings forth bread from the earth.

KIDDUSH – BLESSING OVER THE WINE *

The Hebrew word *kiddush* translates as "sanctification" or "separation." As we drink the wine, we are reminded that we are not of this world but SEPARATED into the kingdom of G-d (John 17:16; John 18:36).

Wine also represents the JOY of the L-rd, and he fills us to overflowing. The first miracle Yeshua performed was turning water into wine. A miracle that defied natural law and revealed his POWER over nature by transforming one element into a completely different element. Our sanctification comes as we are being transformed into a new creation.

Traditionally the man of the home lifts the filled cup of wine and recites the blessing and then each person takes a drink. Each guest may have their own cup of wine.

BLESSING

בָּרוּךְ אַתָּה יהוה אֱלֹהֵינוּ מֶלֶךְ הָעוֹלָם בּוֹרֵא פְּרִי הַגָּפֶן

Baruch a-tah Adonai e-lo-hey-nu me-lech ha-olam bo-rei pe-ri hag-ga-fen.

Blessed are you L-rd our G-d, King of the Universe who creates the fruit of the vine.

* grape juice may be used.

ENJOY DINNER TOGETHER

AFTER DINNER (RECOMMENDED)

PARASHA **DISCUSSION**

The Jewish community reads through the Torah in a yearly cycle called the Parasha. Translated "portion."

We have broken physical bread together and now we break spiritual bread together following the pattern of the first century community. (Acts 2:46; 5:42)

LITURGIES

There are many traditional liturgies, taken from the scriptures, that are recited in the Jewish community on Shabbat. These liturgies connect us in the spiritual realm to our brothers and sisters around the globe who are gathering to celebrate Shabbat and as one voice we lift up these blessings and prayers.

These are provided in the "Liturgies" section that follows.

Prayer is the powerful connection we have into the throne room of heaven. We encourage each Shabbat diner to incorporate prayer for one another as a part of the experience. The prayer of the righteous man is powerful and effective (James 5:16). When we call on the name of the L-rd and "come and pray" He "will listen to you." (Jeremiah 29:12) Shabbat is a time to "bear one another's burdens." (Galatians 6:2)

*These are provided in the "Prayer and Blessings" section that follows.

NOTE: Yehovah and Yahweh are the two common translations of the name of G-d in Hebrew. (יְהוָה) In traditional Judaism this is substituted with Adonai and Hashem. In our translations below you will see Yehovah or Adonai.

The original Hebrew from the scriptures was the full name and is used over 6500 times in the Hebrew Bible.

SHEMA

This ancient prayer is taken from three portions of scripture. Two are in Deuteronomy and one in Numbers. We chant the first line of the Shema to remind us that G-d is sovereign, and G-d is one. He is the only G-d we serve. This prayer is the foundation of our faith.

שְׁמַע יִשְׂרָאֵל יְהֹוָה אֱלֹהֵינוּ יְהֹוָה אֶחָד

בָּרוּךְ שֵׁם כְּבוֹד מַלְכוּתוֹ לְעוֹלָם וָעֶד

Shema Yis-rael Yehovah (Adonai) e-lo-hey-nu Yehovah (Adonai) e-cha. Ba-ruch Shem ka-vod mal-chu-to le-olam va-ed.

Hear O Israel the L-rd our G-d, the L-rd is One

Blessed be the name of his glorious kingdom which is forever and ever.

V'HAVTA (continuation of the Shema)

Deuteronomy 6:5-9

וְאָהַבְתָּ אֵת יְהֹוָה אֱלֹהֶיךָ בְּכָל־לְבָבְךָ וּבְכָל־נַפְשְׁךָ וּבְכָל־מְאֹדֶךָ׃

הַדְּבָרִים הָאֵלֶּה אֲשֶׁר אָנֹכִי מְצַוְּךָ הַיּוֹם עַל־לְבָבֶךָ

וְשִׁנַּנְתָּם לְבָנֶיךָ וְדִבַּרְתָּ בָּם בְּשִׁבְתְּךָ בְּבֵיתֶךָ

וּבְלֶכְתְּךָ בַדֶּרֶךְ וּבְשָׁכְבְּךָ וּבְקוּמֶךָ

וּקְשַׁרְתָּם לְאוֹת עַל־יָדֶךָ וְהָיוּ לְטֹטָפֹת בֵּין עֵינֶיךָ

וּכְתַבְתָּם עַל־מְזוּזֹת בֵּיתֶךָ וּבִשְׁעָרֶיךָ

V'ahavta et Yehovah elohecha b'chol l'vavcha oo'chol nafsh'cha oov-chol me'odecha. V'hayoo had-vareem ha'ayleh asher anochee m'tzav'cha hayom al l'vavecha. V'sheenantam l'vanecha v'deebarta bam b'sheevt'cha b'vaytecha oov'lecht'cha vaderech oov'shachb'cha oov'koomecha ook'shartam l'ot al yadecha v'hayoo l'totafot bein aynecha. Ooch'tavtam al m'zoozot baytecha oovish'arecha.

"Love the L-rd your G-d with all your heart and with all your life and with all your strength. These commandments that I give you today are to be on your hearts. Impress them on your children. Talk about them when you sit at home and when you walk along the road, when you lie down and when you get up. Tie them as reminders on your hands and bind them on your foreheads. Write them on the doorframes of your houses and on your gates." Amen.

V'SHAMRU

Exodus 31:16-17

וְשָׁמְרוּ בְנֵי־יִשְׂרָאֵל אֶת־הַשַּׁבָּת לַעֲשׂוֹת אֶת־הַשַּׁבָּת לְדֹרֹתָם בְּרִית

עוֹלָם׃ בֵּינִי וּבֵין בְּנֵי יִשְׂרָאֵל אוֹת הִוא לְעֹלָם כִּי־שֵׁשֶׁת יָמִים עָשָׂה יְהוָה

אֶת־הַשָּׁמַיִם וְאֶת־הָאָרֶץ וּבַיּוֹם הַשְּׁבִיעִי שָׁבַת וַיִּנָּפַשׁ

V'shamroo v'nay yis'rael et hashabbat la'sot et'hashabbat l'doratim b'reet oo'lam. Benee oovyan b'nay yis'rael 'ot hee l'olam kee sheshat yamen asah Adonai et hashmayeem v'et ha'aratz oovayom hashvee'ee shavat vayeenanfash.

The children of Israel shall keep the Shabbat, observing the Shabbat throughout their generations as an everlasting covenant. It is a sign between me and children of Israel forever, that in six days the L-rd made the heavens and the earth and on the seventh day he ceased from work and rested.

AARONIC BENEDICTION

A traditional blessing giving at the close of our time together.

Numbers 6:24-26

יְבָרֶכְךָ יהוה וְיִשְׁמְרֶךָ:

יָאֵר יהוה פָּנָיו אֵלֶיךָ וִיחֻנֶּךָ:

יִשָּׂא יהוה פָּנָיו אֵלֶיךָ וְיָשֵׂם לְךָ שָׁלוֹם

Y va-reh-cha Adonai v'yish-ma-reh-cha Ya'ayr Adonai pan-av-ay-le-cha v'yi-chu-neh-cha Yis-sa Adonai pan-av-ay-le-cha v'ya-sem le-cha shalom.

The L-rd bless you and keep you. The L-rd make His face to shine upon you and be gracious unto you. The L-rd lift up His countenance upon you and give you peace.

BLESSING OVER THE HOME

Avinu Malkeinu (Our Father and King)

Just as Solomon dedicated the temple to You, I dedicate this home and property to You. (1 Kings 8). It shall be a house of prayer, a house of praise and worship to You my L-rd. May all that is done within the walls and property of this house be used to glorify You L-rd. Like Joshua before me, I declare that "As for me and my house, we will serve the L-rd." (Joshua 24:15). B'shem Yeshua (In the name of Jesus)

PRAYER FOR MARRIAGE

Avinu Malkeinu (Our Father and King)

Just as you brought Adam and Eve together and blessed their union, Father we ask Your blessing on our marriage. We invite

You to be the center of this marriage. We acknowledge that apart from You we can do nothing (John 15:5). We ask You L-rd, to show us how to be considerate of one another's needs and wishes and feelings (Ephesians 5:21-33). Help us to be understanding and forgiving of one another's weaknesses. Help us to walk in forgiveness always remembering that You have forgiven us (Ephesians 4:32) Help us to show Your mercy and grace to each other and to keep no record of past hurts or failures (1 Corinthians 13:5). Thank you, Father, for my spouse. We believe You have called us together to glorify You and serve You. B'shem Yeshua (In the name of Jesus)

PRAYER FOR CHILDREN

Avinu Malkeinu (Our Father and King)

Make your face shine upon my children and be gracious unto them. Lift up Your countenance upon them and give them peace. (Numbers 6:23-26) I pray that they will love You, L-rd, with all their heart, with all their soul and with all their mind, might and strength and love their neighbor as themselves. (Deuteronomy 6:5, Mark 12:30, Matthew 22:37-39) Just as Samuel was dedicated to You as a child, so I give my children back to You. I pray that my children will seek You, L-rd, and shall not lack any good thing. (Psalm 34:10) Teach them how to grow in wisdom and stature and favor with you and favor with all people. (Luke 2:52) B'shem Yeshua (In the name of Jesus)

BLESSING FOR WIFE

Avinu Malkeinu (Our Father and King)

I thank you for my wife. I honor her. She is more precious to me than all the wealth in this world. I trust her with my whole heart. Bless her with strength and resourcefulness as she cares for our family. Bless her that she may hear our children rise up and call her blessed as she trusts in you and walks in the fear of the L-rd. Pour out your blessings upon her. Reward her with all the things she deserves. (Proverbs 31:10-31) B'shem Yeshua (In the name of Jesus)

BLESSING FOR HUSBAND

Avinu Malkeinu (Our Father and King)

I thank you for my husband. His trust is firmly in You. Because of You, he is steady in the storms of life. He is strong and courageous. He is a man of integrity who always seeks to do what is righteous. My heart is drawn to his kindness and compassion for others. He leads and loves our family well. He is honored among men and makes wise decisions. Give him increase in all he does. (Psalm 112:1-9) B'shem Yeshua (In the name of Jesus)

A TRADITIONAL BLESSING OVER SONS AND DAUGHTERS

In Genesis 48, Jacob laid his hand upon his grandsons Ephraim and Manasseh and gave them the blessing of a double portion. It has become a custom in the home each Shabbat to bless the boys and the girls of the home as Jacob did.

For Boys begin:

יְשִׂמְךָ אֱלֹהִים כְּאֶפְרַיִם וְכִמְנַשֶּׁה

Yis'm'cha Elohim k'Efrayim v'ch'Menashe.

May you be like Ephraim and Mehnashe

For Girls begin:

יְשִׂמֵךְ אֱלֹהִים כְּשָׂרָה, כְּרִבְקָה, כְּרָחֵל, וּכְלֵאָה.

Yis'meych Elohim k'Sarah, Rivkah, Rachel v'Leah.

May you be like Sarah, Rebecca, Rachel, and Leah

Then complete for all:

יְבָרֶכְךָ יְהֹנָה וְיִשְׁמְרֶךָ

Yivarechecha (Yehovah) Adonai v'yishmerecha

May G-s bless you and protect you.

יָאֵר יְהוָה פָּנָיו אֵלֶיךָ וִיחֻנֶּךָ

Ya'er (Yehovah) Adonai panav eilecha vichuneka

May G-d show you favor and be gracious to you.

יִשָּׂא יְהוָה פָּנָיו אֵלֶיךָ וְיָשֵׂם לְךָ שָׁלוֹם

Yisa Adonai panav eilecha v'yasem lecha shalom

May G-d show you kindness and grant you peace.

CHALLAH RECIPE

CHALLAH IN A HURRY

- 6 cups of bread flour
- 4 ½ teaspoon yeast
- Dash of kosher salt
- 4 eggs
- 1 ½ cups hot water
- 2 sticks of butter (softened)
- ¾ cups of sugar (or honey)
- Sesame seeds or poppy seeds (optional)

1. Mix 5 ½ cups of flour in a large bowl. Add yeast and salt. Stir to mix.

2. In a separate bowl mix together melted butter, water, sugar, 3 beaten eggs.

3. Pour wet ingredients into the dry ingredients. Mix to incorporate wet ingredients until dough holds together.

4. When a ball forms, dump onto lightly floured surface and begin to knead until smooth. Pray over the bread and the guests who will share this bread.

5. Split the dough into two large pieces. Split the two large pieces into three pieces each. Roll each third into ¾ inch thick ropes and braid the three strands together. Repeat with second large piece. Placed the shaped dough onto a greased cookie sheet. Let rise in a warm place until doubled in size.

6. Brush dough with remaining beaten egg. Add sesame seeds or poppy seeds if desired.

7. Bake in a preheated 325-degree oven for 20-30 minutes until golden.

COOL RISE CHALLAH

(From Food52.com)

- 6-7 cups all-purpose flour
- 4 ½ teaspoon active dry yeast
- ½ cup sugar
- 1 ½ teaspoon salt
- 1 1/3 cups hot tap water
- 8 tablespoons unsalted butter, softened.
- 4 eggs at room temperature, plus one more at baking time
- Splash of milk
- Oil for the bowl

1. Combine 2 cups of flour with the yeast, sugar, and salt in a large bowl and stir well. Add softened butter and stir again.

2. Add the hot tap water and beat with the paddle attachment of an electric mixer at medium speed for 2 minutes until well mixed and elastic.

3. Add the eggs and 1 ½ cups more flour. Beat on medium-high speed for 1 minute or until thick and elastic.

4. If you are using a stand mixer, switch to a dough hook on low speed and gradually stir in enough of remaining flour to make a soft dough that leaves the sides of bowl. Alternatively, stir in the last bit of flour with a wooden spoon and turn the dough out onto a floured board.

5. Knead 5 to 10 minutes, adding additional flour as needed, until it is smooth, elastic. Place the dough in a large, lightly oiled bowl, turning it over once to fully coat with oil. Cover with a tea towel and let rise for 20 minutes.

6. After 20 minutes, divide the dough into two even pieces. Set one aside and cover with a dish towel. Gently roll the

first piece into a fat log and divide again into as many pieces as you want to braid. Roll each small piece into a snake, aiming for equal length and thickness. Pinch the ends of the snakes together and braid until you reach the other ends. Tuck both ends securely under the loaf. Repeat with other half then set both on parchment sheet and refrigerate for 2-24 hours.

7. To bake, bring loaves to room temperature and preheat oven to 350 degrees.

8. Beat an egg in a small dish with splash of milk and gently brush over the loaves. Bake for 35-40 minutes until the loaves are a rich golden brown.

To my Jewish Friends...What is Work?

Passed down through the centuries, the Jewish people have had the sages provide many definitions of work to prevent them from violating the Shabbat. Work has many interpretations. In this book, I have described some of those interpretations. Most importantly, I have taken a strong stance against defining work for others. My belief is that each one must have a revelation from G-d. What I define as work may very well have some differences from how another defines work. As a teacher of the Word of G-d, I have a responsibility to teach people how to hear the voice of the L-rd for themselves. I therefore shy away from trying to legislate the details of every command of scripture.

I am always appreciative of other viewpoints, and I try to be open minded so I can learn.

When the Jews came back from exile in Babylon, a Torah scroll was found and read. Upon reading the scroll the people were cut to the heart for their disobedience and understood why G-d sent the nation into exile. They were quick to repent and decided they could never let that happen again. As they began to obey the Torah commands, they decided to construct what they called a "fence" around the Torah. These were additional rules and commands in order to put a fence between their obedience and disobedience. Many of the fences were built from the right heart and reason-to prevent disobedience- however they consistently showed man's imprint. These fences became large and cumbersome. When we add to G-d's word, we will inevitably create a system that is fallen in its nature. In my opinion, the system created over the centuries to prevent people from working on Shabbat is not what G-d had in mind when He stated we should not work.

Years ago, in the Unites States, congress enacted a law to collect an income tax on all working Americans. In order to enforce the law, they created an agency, the Internal Revenue Service, to determine what counted as income. The IRS spends countless hours and money writing thousands upon thousands of pages of code with the single purpose of defining income.

This is similar to the laws given by the sages. G-d gave a command not to work on Shabbat and the sages became the agency by which work was defined.

The scriptures do not give an exhaustive list of what is allowed when it comes to work. There are some references from which we can draw conclusions.

We are told in Exodus 34:21 and Numbers 15:32-36 to avoid field labor. At the time of these writings field labor included harvesting, planting, gathering or essentially the agricultural work in which most were engaged. This could mean the work of the field specifically, or could also mean the work that is being done the other six days of the week.

For example, we are told to avoid treading the winepress and loading animals in Nehemiah 13:15-18. This certainly could be a discussion about the labor of producing food and drink as well as about preparing for the work of the next day by getting the animals ready.

In Isaiah 58:13, Jeremiah 17:22 and Amos 8:5 we are told to avoid the carrying on of business such as buying and selling of goods. These verses make clear that to buy and sell on Shabbat is considered a type of work since it is the same thing that merchants did for their survival the other six days of the week. However, in context, these verses seemed to indicate the merchants were taking advantage of the crowds on Shabbat and thus, working and being selfish. Much more was going on here beyond just buying an item on Saturday.

A very real principal emerges out of these verses. Work on Shabbat is to provide for ourselves as we do the other six days of the week. Shabbat is the day we remember G-d is the provider and the sustainer of all things. He is the one we are to depend on and with Him we are to co-labor. On the Shabbat, we find our rest in what He has done. For example, in the desert G-d provided *manna* on the sixth day that would be enough to last through the Shabbat. They needed to survive but that provision of His grace and their obedience would provide enough to last for two days. In other words, work on Shabbat is that which detracts from the L-rd being the provider and places our trust elsewhere.

FIRE

We are told in Exodus 35:2-3 to not kindle a fire on Shabbat. This command has been used to create a number of rules that include not driving on Shabbat or pushing an elevator button on Shabbat. The context of the verses tells us how to interpret this passage. It comes in the middle of G-d giving the instructions for the building of the tabernacle. Building the tabernacle was a massive construction project and required crafts of carpentry, sewing, metal work and blacksmithing to name just a few. When we look at the instructions we see that the melting down of gold, silver and bronze was going to be a significant part of the work. For example,

Exodus 25:12-13

You are to cast four rings of gold for it, and place them in its four feet. Two rings will be on one side, and two rings on the other side. Also make poles of acacia wood and overlay them with gold.

Exodus 26:37

You are also to make for the screen five pillars of acacia, and overlay them with gold. Their hooks are to be made of gold, and you are to cast five bases of bronze for them.

These verses and so many more explain that the melting and shaping of metal was going to be required and fire was the tool to do the job. Exodus 38:28-29 explains the sheer volume of metal. Approximately 3-4 metric tons were used.

As G-d told Moses to give the people the instructions on how to build the tabernacle, he also reminded them that they have six days to do this work. On the seventh day they are not to light a fire in their home and do this work. That is the true context. G-d does not and did not forbid anyone from lighting a fire to warm your home or cook your meal. This command is specific to the metal workers being reminded to stop their work on the Shabbat.

The Orthodox Jewish community is faithful to follow the traditions of Rabbis as have been handed down throughout many generations. Those of us who are followers of Messiah Yeshua would do well to learn from the example of this community when it comes to passing on from one generation to the next. Those that I have personally met within the Orthodox community have a deep desire to serve, honor and please G-d. To that end, when it comes to Shabbat the Rabbis have created hundreds of rules that must be followed. These rules are codified in the Mishna and the Talmud. These works are considered the written explanation of the "oral law." Thereby, these are not suggestions but rather, for the Jew living in the Orthodox community, these are the very words of G-d.

To my friends in the Jewish community, I personally thank you for guarding and keeping Shabbat. However, I would ask that you review the written Torah of Moses to see that the words given by him from G-d are the only rules that are needed for us. In the Tanakh we have all we need to find the right path to G-d. G-d loves us and left us with His word and His Spirit that we may come to know and follow Him. He is our teacher and will forever show us His way when questions arise.

As a teacher and leader of a community of faith, I understand the desire for order and even submission to G-d given authority. However, I encourage you to search the scriptures and see that the G-d of heaven has already given us the words of life to follow. Rabbis can provide aid without it being binding.

Deuteronomy 31:9-13

*Moses **wrote down** this Torah and gave it to the kohanim, the sons of Levi who carry the Ark of the Covenant of Adonai, and to all the elders of Israel.*

*Then Moses commanded them saying, "At the end of every seven years, in the set time of the year of cancelling debts, during the feast of Sukkot, when all Israel comes to appear before Adonai your G-d in the place He chooses, you are to read **this** Torah before them in their hearing. Gather the people—the men and women and little ones, and the outsider within your town gates— **so they may hear and so they may learn, and they will fear** Adonai your G-d and **take care to do all the words of this Torah.** So their children, who have not known, will hear and learn to fear Adonai your G-d—all the days you live on the land you are about to cross over the Jordan to possess."*

Deuteronomy 13:1-5

*Whatever I command you, you must take care to do—**you are not to add to it or take away from it.** "Suppose a prophet or a dreamer of dreams rises up among you and gives you a sign or wonder, and the sign or wonder he spoke to you comes true, while saying, 'Let's follow other G-ds'—that you have not known, and— 'Let's serve them!' You must not listen to the words of that prophet or that dreamer of dreams—for Adonai your G-d is testing you, to find out whether you love Adonai your G-d with all your heart and with all your soul. Adonai your G-d you will* *follow and Him you will fear. His mitzvot you will keep, to His voice you will listen, Him you will serve and to Him you will cling.*

Deuteronomy 17:14-18

When you come to the land that Adonai your G-d is giving you, possess it and dwell in it, and you say, 'I will set a king over me, like all the nations around me,' you will indeed set over yourselves a king, whom Adonai your G-d chooses. One from among your brothers will be appointed as king over you—you may not put a foreigner over you, who is not your brother. Only he should not multiply horses for himself or make the people return to Egypt to multiply horses, because Adonai has said to you, "You must never go back that way again." Nor should he multiply wives for himself, so that his heart does not turn aside, nor multiply much silver and gold for himself.

*"Now when he sits on the throne of his kingdom, he is to write for himself a copy of **this Torah** on a scroll, from what is before the Levitical kohanim. It will remain with him, **and he will read in it all the days of his life,** in order to learn to fear Adonai his G-d and keep all the words of this Torah and these statutes. Then his heart will not be exalted above his brothers, and he will not turn from the commandment to the right or to the left—so that he may prolong his days in his kingship, he and his sons, in the midst of Israel.*

As you can see, G-d left no doubt that Moses wrote down and passed on everything that we were to have today as the "word of G-d." Any additions to the Torah by way of Oral Law are traditions of men and may be useful but are not required by G-d. For any of my Jewish brethren who have made it this far in the book or just flipped to this section, I ask you to strongly consider the written words of Moses regarding Shabbat. Study the actual words of Moses in Torah and the words of the prophets and see for yourself that G-d has a beautiful, life-giving and freedom plan for Shabbat. Enjoy the gift!

HEBREW TERMS AND DEFINITIONS

Pronunciations

In the transliteration of the Hebrew text, most of the sounds are to be pronounced as in English, however, please note the following:

• The apostrophe (') is used to indicate a reduced vowel similar to the "e" in courtesy, e.g. l'hodot

a and ah = ah, as in father

ai = i as in sky

e = eh as in bed

i = ee as in see

u =oo as in food

ch = as in "Scottish" loch

tz = ts as in boats

ei = ay as in plate

o =oh as in go

Here are some of the words and definitions used in this book that may be unfamiliar to some.

Yeshua: Jesus

G-d: a dash is inserted to show honor to the name of G-d. This is not required by scripture but is used to cause one to pause and reflect for a moment on the unique nature of our G-d.

Adonai: L-rd

Yahweh or Yehovah: the Hebrew name G-d used to identify Himself in the scriptures. The four letters, יְהֹוָה ,yud hey vav hey, are used over 6800 times in the Bible. The pronunciation of the name has not been used in Judaism for almost 2000 years. However, vowel markings were added to the Hebrew script between 600 and 800 C.E by the Masorites. The vowel markings have spurred the debate on the pronunciation. In this book we use Yehovah primarily but Yahweh occasionally.

HaShem: The Name. Is used primarily in Jewish circles as they have been taught that the name of the L-rd is either not known or cannot be spoken. Neither of those reasons is listed in the Bible.

Ekklesia: Call out ones, Called out to rule. This is the Greek word used in the Septuagint and the New Testament meaning assembly or congregation. This word eventually got translated to "church." However, it does not mean church and never did. Church as a description of the body of Messiah was an invention of the Roman rulership.

Shema: Hear, Listen, Obey.

Baruch: Bless.

Shabbat: Sabbath, Rest.

Shaul (Saul) | Paul: Saul was the Hebrew name for the apostle to the Gentiles who wrote many of the letters of the New Testament. Paul was his given Roman name, as he was a roman citizen. He did not change his name from Shaul to Paul after he was born again as some have claimed. In this book we use Rabbi Shaul, Saul, Paul and the Apostle Paul interchangeably.

Torah: The first five books of the Bible. Sometimes called the books of Moses as he is considered the primary author.

Tanakh: This is an acronym for what is commonly referred to as the "Old Testament." Although in most Bibles today this consist of 39 books, in the Hebrew Bible and the original works it was comprise of twenty-two books. These combined some, such as first and second Kings, Chronicles and Samuel. The same books are in both divisions. These are divided into three parts: The word Tanakh is an acronym of these divisions: The five books of the

Torah ("teaching"); the Nevi'im ("prophets"); and the Ketuvim ("writings"). The order of the Hebrew Bible is not the same as the Greek canonical collection, now used in many English translations.

New Testament: Sometimes called the New Covenant which is an inaccurate term for the combined writings of the New Testament. Some refer to these as the apostolic writings. They contain twenty-seven books; the four Canonical gospels, Acts of the Apostles, twenty-one Epistles or letters and the Book of Revelation.

The Bible itself never refers to itself as an Old or New Testament. The Bible refers to itself as Scripture and the word of G-d. Removing the division of Old and New from our minds can help us to rightly discern meanings of passages. We call this "One Book One Story."

Ruach HaKodesh: The Holy Spirit

Jeff Friedlander

THE FEASTS OF THE L-RD

SPRING FEASTS

Pesach (Passover) Nisan 14

Passover remembers the miraculous exodus of the Israelites out of Egyptian slavery and our exodus out of sin through the blood of the lamb.

Chag Hamatzot (Unleavened Bread) Nisan 15-21

A seven-day period of not eating bread containing leaven.

Sefirat Haomer (Counting the Omer) Nisan 15-Sivan 5

A fifty-day period between Passover and Shavuot.

Yom Habikkurim (Day of First Fruits) Nisan 17

A celebration of the spring harvest.

SUMMER FEASTS

Shavuot (Pentecost) Sivan 6

Celebration of the Torah given to Moses on Mt. Sinai and the pouring out of the *Ruach HaKodesh* (Holy Spirit) in Jerusalem.

FALL FEASTS

Yom Teruah (Day of Trumpets/Rosh Hashanah)
Tishri 1

A celebration of the announcing of the coming King. It is also the civil new year for Israel.

Yom Kippur (Day of Atonement)
Tishri 10

The annual day when the Kohen Gadol (High Priest) entered the temple to make atonement for people of Israel. Celebrated today remembering Messiah and the blood atonement He made for all who believe.

Sukkot (Feast of Tabernacles)

Hebrew Month: Tishri 15-21
A seven-day celebration of remembering the huts Israel lived in during their forty-year sojourn in the desert. Celebrated today by building sukkot (temporary dwellings) in which meals are eaten in for the week. As believers in Messiah, we celebrate in anticipation of the day Messiah returns to "tabernacle" with us for eternity.

Hoshanah Rabah (7th Day of Sukkot) Tishri 21

The closing of the great feasts of Booths and a holy convocation.

END NOTES AND REFERENCES

Introduction

1. Eusebius, *Life of Constantine* Vol. III Ch. XVIII Life of Constantine (Book III) (Catholic Encyclopedia)

2. *Codex Justinianus* 3.12.3, trans. Philip Schaff, History of the Christian Church, 5th ed. New York, 1902, 3:380, note 1.

Chapter 1

1. "Messianic Judaism in Antiquity and in the Modern Era." Pages 21-36 in Introduction to Messianic Judaism: Its Ecclesial Context and Biblical Foundations. Edited by David J. Rudolph and Joel Willitts. Grand Rapids: Zondervan, 2013.

Chapter 2

1. Ephesians 2:14-18

For He is our shalom, the One who made the two into one and broke down the middle wall of separation. Within His flesh He made powerless the hostility—the law code of mitzvot contained in regulations. He did this in order to create within Himself one new man from the two groups, making shalom, and to reconcile both to God in one body through the cross—by which He put the hostility to death. And He came and proclaimed shalom to you who were far away and shalom to those who were near—

for through Him we both have access to the Father by the same Ruach.

2. The spirit of *Mammon* is real and carries with it destruction. I encourage you to pray over the influence this spirit may have in your life. To learn more we recommend the book Wealth, Riches & Money, *Craig Hill and Earl Pitts, Family Foundations Publishing (2001)*

3. Deuteronomy 8:11-14

"Take care that you do not forget Adonai your God by not keeping His mitzvot, ordinances and statutes that I am commanding you today. Otherwise, when you have eaten and are full and have built good houses and lived in them, and when your herds and flocks multiply, and silver and gold multiplies for you and all that is yours multiplies, then your heart will be haughty and you will forget Adonai your God. He brought you out from the land of Egypt, from the house of slavery.

Chapter 3

1. https://www.breakingisraelnews.com/120106/noahide-court-Messiah-nations-sabbath/

Chapter 4

1. Asher Ginsberg, poet, philosopher, 1856-1927: *https://mishkan.org/rabbishawn/blog/more-than-jews-have-kept-shabbat-shabbat-has-kept-the-jews-1*

Chapter 5

1. Benjamin Franklin; *On the Constitution (1787) https://www.faithgateway.com/the-prayer-that-saved-the-constitution/*

Chapter 8

1. Tigay, Jeffery H. (1998). "Shavua". *Mo'adei Yisra'el:* Time and Holy Days in the Biblical and Second Commonwealth Periods *(Heb.), ed. Jacob S. Licht*: 22–23.

Friedman, Allen (September 2008). "Unnatural Time: Its History and Theological Significance". *The Torah U-Madda Journal.* **15**: 104–105.

2. https://eaglesanddragonspublishing.com/ancient-everyday-the-days-and-the-weeks-in-ancient-rome

3. M'Clatchie, "*Notes and Queries on China and Japan*" (edited by Dennys), Vol 4, Nos 7, 8, p.100.

4. IBID P.99

5. Ronald Dart: "Born to Win, From Passover to Easter". 2003, 2006 https://www.cogwriter.com/crucifixionweek.htm

6. https://Biblehub.com/commentaries/clarke/mark/2.htm

7. The Whole Works of Jeremey Taylor, *Vol. IX, p416 (R. Heber's Edition, Vol.XII, p.416)*

7. Antiquities of the Christian Church, Vol. II, Book XX, chap. 3, Sec. 1, 66.1137, 1138.

8. Dialogues on the L-rd's Day, p. 189. London: 1701, by Dr. T.H. Morer.

9. Geschichte des Sonntags, pp. 13, 14.

10. Gieseler's Church History, Vol. 1, ch. 2, par. 30, p. 93.

11. The Oxyrhynchus Papyri, pt. L, p. 3, Logion 2, verse 4-11 (London: Offices of the Egypt Exploration Fund, 1898)

Chapter 9

1. *Cave William, D.D.* Primitive Christianity: or the Religion of the Ancient Christians in the First Ages of the Gospel. *1840 edition revised by H. Cary. Oxford, London, pp. 84-85).*

2. Tertullian. Against Marcion, Book IV, Chapter 12. Excerpted from Ante-Nicene Fathers, Volume 3. Edited by Philip Schaff, D.D., LL.D. American Edition, 1885. Online Edition Copyright © 2005 by K. Knight.

3. Bacchiocchi S. Anti-Judaism and the Origin of Sunday. The Pontifical Gregorian University Press, Rome, 1975, p. 62.

4. https://www.catholic.com/magazine/print-edition/marcionism

5.. *Justin Martryr* First Apology 67, *Justin Martryr.* Dialogue with Trypho, 21. *Justin Martryr.* Dialogue with Trypho, 23. *Justin Martryr.* Dialogue with Trypho,12:3.

6. Iganatius, Epistle to the Magnesians, complete but in particular Chapter 3. https://www.sacred-texts.com/bib/lbob/lbob19.htm

7. *"The Sabbath Day, Sunday, and the Eighth Day." St. Sophia Greek Orthodox Church Bellingham, Washington. http://www.saintsophias.org/the-sabbath-day.html viewed 10/30/14*

8. O'Leary, *"The Syriac Church and Fathers,"* pp. 83, 84. *Coltheart JF.* The Sabbath of G-d Through the Centuries. *Leaves-of-Autumn Books, Inc. Payson, Arizona, 1954.*

http://www.giveshare.org/churchhistory/sabbaththrucenturies.h
tml 6/24/06).

9. The canons of the council of Laodicea, 364 CE.
https://sabbathsentinel.org/canons-from-laodicea/

10. https://www.ccel.org/ccel/schaff/npnf210.v.ix.html

11. *J.N. Andrews,* History of the Sabbath, *pp.146 PDF*

12. *Codex Justinianus 3.12.3, trans. Philip Schaff,* History of
the Christian Church, *5th ed. (New York, 1902), 3:380, note 1.*

13. IBID

14. *Eusebius,* Life of Constantine *3. 17-18, Theodoret,* Church
History *1.9 Gelasius,* Church History *2.37.10*

15. The Faith of Millions, Reverend John A. O'Brien, PH. D.,
4th Edition, copyright 1938, published by "Our Sunday
Visitor," Huntington, Ind., page 147

Chapter 10

1. Psalm 124:1

A psalm of David.
The earth is ADONAI's and all that fills it
the world, and those dwelling on it.

2. https://www.cdc.gov/nchs/fastats/unmarried-childbearing.htm

3. Matthew 5:32

But I say to you that everyone who divorces his wife, except for
sexual immorality, makes her commit adultery; and whoever
marries a divorced woman commits adultery.

4. Some of these are an adaptation from CMJ Ministries. Others are from Be One Ministries and some are a combination of several different practiced blessings.

Chapter 11

1. Exodus 20:8-11

Remember Yom Shabbat, to keep it holy. You are to work six days, and do all your work, but the seventh day is a Shabbat to Adonai your God. In it you shall not do any work—not you, nor your son, your daughter, your male servant, your female servant, your cattle, nor the outsider that is within your gates. For in six days Adonai made heaven and earth, the sea, and all that is in them, and rested on the seventh day. Thus Adonai blessed Yom Shabbat, and made it holy.

2. www.blueletterBible.org/lang/lexicon/lexicon.cfm?strongs=G266 3 Thayer's Greek Lexicon THAYER'S GREEK LEXICON, Electronic Database.
Copyright © 2002, 2003, 2006, 2011 by Biblesoft, Inc.

3. 1 Peter 1: 8-12

*Though you have not seen Him, you love Him. And even though you don't see Him now, you trust Him and are filled with a joy that is glorious beyond words, **receiving the outcome of your faith—the salvation of your souls.** The prophets, who spoke about the grace that was to be yours, searched for this salvation and investigated carefully. They were trying to find out the time and circumstances the Ruach of Messiah within them was indicating, when predicting the sufferings in store for Messiah and the glories to follow. It was revealed to them that they were providing these messages not to themselves but to you. These* *messages have now been announced to you through those who proclaimed the Good News to you by the Ruach ha-Kodesh, sent from heaven. Even angels long to catch a glimpse of these things.*

4. Deuteronomy 6:24-25

Adonai commanded us to do all these statutes, to fear Adonai our God—for our good always, to keep us alive, as is the case this day. It will be righteousness to us, if we take care to do all this commandment before Adonai our God, just as He has commanded us.'

Chapter 12

1. www.rand.org/pubs/research_reports/RR1791.html

2. www.tuck.com/economics-of-sleep/

3. www.worldometers.info/world-population/

4. https://londonimageinstitute.com/how-much-of-communication-is-nonverbal/

5. https://neurosciencenews.com/binge-watching-neuroscience-14663/

6. www.nbcnews.com/better/health/what-happens-your-brain-when-you-binge-watch-tv-series-ncna816991

Chapter 13

1. Isaiah 55:8-11

For My thoughts are not your thoughts, nor are your ways My ways." It is a declaration of Adonai. "For as the heavens are higher than earth, so are My ways higher than your ways, and My thoughts than your thoughts. For as the rain and snow come down from heaven, and do not return there without having watered the earth, making it bring forth and sprout, giving seed to sow and bread to eat, so My word will be that goes out from My mouth. It will not return to Me in vain, but will accomplish what I intend, and will succeed in what I sent it for.

2. www.theatlantic.com/business/archive/2014/08/where-the-five-day-workweek-came-from/378870/

3. www.chabad.org/library/article_cdo/aid/95906/jewish/Melacha-A-Unique-Definition-of-Work.htm

4. https://en.wikipedia.org/wiki/Activities_prohibited_on_Shabbat

5. http://torah.org.il/learning/halacha/classes/class379.html

Additional references were used from:

As per Talmud Shabbat 6a., Code of Jewish Law, Orach Chaim, 345:7. Babylonian Talmud Eruvin 22b.

Chapter 14

1. https://torah.org/torah-portion/weekly-halacha-5771-bamidbar/

2.. https://Biblehub.com/commentaries/numbers/15-32.html

3. Proverbs 16:18

Pride goes before destruction and a haughty spirit before a fall.

Chapter 16

1. Frithjof Schuon, Logic and Transcendence
https://www.goodreads.com/quotes/tag/absolute-truth

Other material referenced in various places

Heylyn, The History of the Sabbath, *1613. Brewer, Ebenezer Cobham (1900).* Dictionary of Phrase and Fable: Giving the Derivation, Source, Or Origin of Common Phrases, Allusions, and Words that Have a Tale to Tell (3 ed.). *Cassell. p. 1070. OCLC 258268902.*

Strand, *op. cit.,* citing Charles J. Hefele, A History of the Councils of the Church, 2 [Edinburgh, 1876] 316)."

http://cgi.org/who-changed-the-sabbath-to-sunday/

Jeff Friedlander

The Hebraic Institute offers a series of courses designed to advance students' Biblical Literacy and Hebraic Thinking. Each course provides a larger context of Biblical understanding and perspective. As the students complete each course their knowledge of G-d, their experience with Him and community and their desire for the Word of G-d will grow.

For more information, visit www.beonetoday.org

Jeff Friedlander

About the Author

Rabbi Jeff Friedlander is a Jewish believer in Yeshua (Jesus). Rabbi Jeff and his wife Sherri have been married since 1990. They began their journey together at the University of Georgia. After graduating with a B.S. in Hospitality Management, they were married and now have four adult children, four grandchildren and Sherri's dog, Rosie. Yes, the dog is that important. Dedicating their first year of marriage to the L-rd, they attended a ministry leadership program called The Master's Commission in Phoenix, Arizona. In addition to the Berean Bible College curriculum, each student participated in practical hands-on ministry.

Rabbi Jeff received a Christian Worker's License and was ordained through the International Assemblies of God Fellowship as a minister. Rabbi Jeff also attended Rabbinical training and was ordained as a Messianic Rabbi and Teacher. In addition to ministry, he owned and managed several businesses for over two decades.

Today he leads Be One Ministries and Fellowship in Birmingham, Alabama.

www.beonetoday.org

Made in the USA
Columbia, SC
05 December 2022

72762781R00128